Jamil Nasser

Fine Printing

Its Inception, Development and Practice

Jamil Nasser

Fine Printing
Its Inception, Development and Practice

ISBN/EAN: 9783337249922

Printed in Europe, USA, Canada, Australia, Japan

Cover: Foto ©Andreas Hilbeck / pixelio.de

More available books at **www.hansebooks.com**

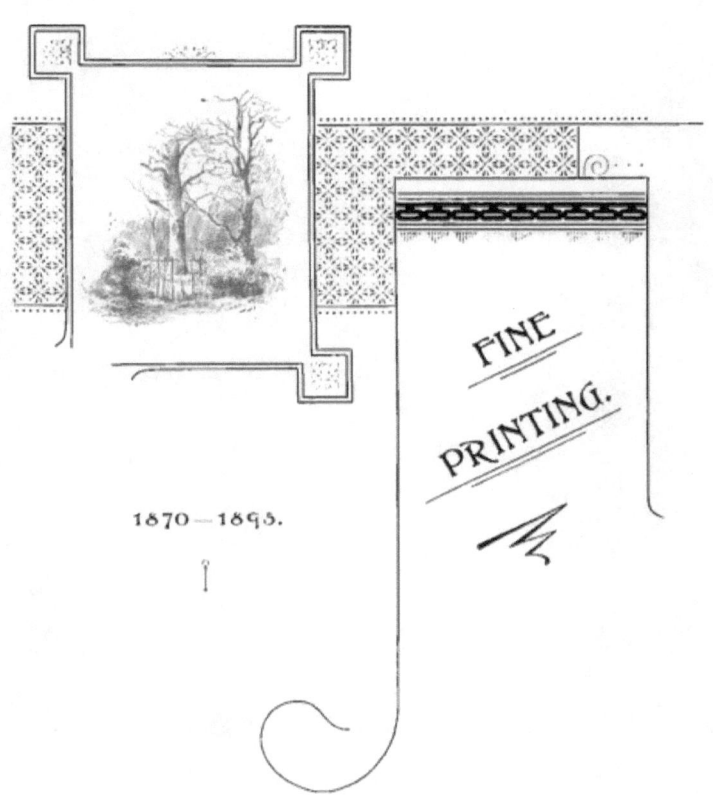

FINE PRINTING.

1870—1895.

FROM PHOTO BY PAYNE JENNINGS.

FINE PRINTING:

ITS INCEPTION, DEVELOPMENT, AND PRACTICE.

BY

GEORGE JOYNER.

WITH TWELVE ARTISTIC SUPPLEMENTS ILLUSTRATING THE TENDENCY OF FINE WORK.

LONDON:
PRINTED AND PUBLISHED BY COOPER AND BUDD,
HIGH STREET, PECKHAM.
1895.

PRINTED BY
COOPER AND BUDD, PECKHAM, LONDON, S.E.

CONTENTS.

	PAGE
INTRODUCTION	v

CHAPTER I.
THE INCEPTION OF FINE PRINTING	3

CHAPTER II.
FINE PRINTING IN THE UNITED KINGDOM: ITS COMMENCEMENT AND PROGRESS	23

CHAPTER III.
FINE COMPOSITION FROM TWO STANDPOINTS	47
I. *The Employer:*	
The Order Sheet	50
Classification of Borders and Types	53
Reference Book of Material	55
II. *The Compositor:*	
Artistic or Good Taste	61
Proportion of Display	62
Uniformity and Contrast of Type Faces	64
Composing Work for Black or Colour	65
Spacing	65
Rising of Quads and Spaces near Blocks	67
Finish of Details	67

CHAPTER IV.
FINE PRESSWORK	73
I. *Its Management:*	
The Order Sheet	76
Arrangement with a view to Expedition	77
Drying Racks	78
Machinery for Fine Presswork	78
Supply of Rollers	81
Papers for Fine Work	81
II. *Its Practice:*	
Fine Work at Platen Machine	84
Fine Work at Cylinder Machine	90
Making Ready Half-tone Engravings	95
Making Ready Wood Engravings	100
Embossing	104
Treatment of Rollers	106

APPENDIX	110

EXAMPLES.

	NEXT TO PAGE
Circular: Style of 1877 ...	12
Specimen of Wood Engraving ...	20
Ornamental Panel Style ...	28
Typical German Style	36
Typical American Style ...	44
British New Style, 1888 ...	52
Specimen of Half-tone Engraving	60
Chromo-Typography: "Azaleas"	68
Geometrical Arrangement of Rule and Border	76
Grouping Display ...	84
Specimen of Embossing ...	92
Specimen of Swain's Photo-Chromotype	100

INTRODUCTION.

OSSIBLY in no other section has the modern advance in the Art of Printing been more pronounced than in that which embraces book, periodical, and job typography in its fine or artistic aspect. In other spheres of the art, progress has been characterised more by the introduction of ingenious mechanism for accomplishing larger and speedier production than by higher excellence in the work or the necessity for increased artistic perception in the workman. It would be altogether undesirable to institute comparison between the different developments in the several branches of the craft that have been collectively instrumental in advancing the Art of Printing to the honourable position of the greatest productive agent known to the world, and rendering it supreme amongst crafts in benefiting the human race. Each has its own distinctive merit. But there is an especial interest attaching to a development whose influence has lifted the job work of this country from a condition of chronic flatness and brought out new and highly artistic typographical qualities in the proper application of which the compositor and the pressman attain a higher status. That development is technically comprehended in the title of this work: "Fine Printing."

As is now well known, the forward movement in Fine Printing had its origin in America. The art had there reached a remarkable state of beauty and efficiency, especially in job work, several years before its influence was apparent in this country. The excellent productions of American craftsmen, which came to British printers through various channels, were instrumental eventually, however, in bringing our typographers to see that, in comparison, their work lacked many—if not most—of the "requisites pertaining to Art." If we accept this influence merely in the nature of a reciprocation for the services rendered many years ago to the craft of the New World by such Englishmen as WINDT and CRATE, and to go still further back, by the great FRANKLIN himself, who "learned his trade in the printing office of Samuel Palmer, in London, in 1724, and two years later entered into business as a printer in Philadelphia,"[*] in view of the present achievements of Fine Printing, we cannot but be struck with its amplitude.

Following closely on the freshness and freedom of American typographical influence, yet another powerful agent appealed to the newly-awakened artistic faculties of British printers, namely, the somewhat formal but exquisite work of the Fatherland. There is no doubt that, to a great extent, this second influence exercised a most wholesome restraint on this country's craftsmen; for their productions were kept comparatively free from the eccentricity and extravagance that during a subsequent period characterised some of their American *confrères'* work.

---

[*] "The Pentateuch of Printing," by William Blades.

INTRODUCTION.

From the American and German styles, and material that came principally from the type-foundries of those countries, British typographers in course of time evolved a style whose fuller development renders it not an unworthy claimant for the occupancy of that "lovely field of design" which our great Art critic, JOHN RUSKIN, considers open to the manipulators of decorative type. Interchange of work in the "Printers' International Specimen Exchange" and influential trade journals have given extended effect to that style. And who shall say that modern British fine typography has not had some share in bringing about the similarity that to-day exists between the first-class work of America and Great Britain? May it not also be from the same cause that German printers have been induced to relinquish some of their typographical formality?

However that may be, the style of British Fine Printing, in the main, more successfully combined the elements of art and practicability than the other two styles; and, after all, fine typography, like the Drama, "must succeed as a business affair in order not to fail as an Art." Fine Printing has its commercial value if judiciously managed. Guesswork in matters connected with the "Art Preservative" is proverbial; but fine typography does not lend itself agreeably to guesswork, either in the estimating or in the carrying out. To make fine work financially and technically successful it is necessary to get through semblances to facts in both particulars.

Concerning the scope of this book, the author does not claim that it is an absolutely exhaustive treatise on Fine Printing. CARLYLE, in his essay on SCOTT, says: "In all things which a man engages in, there is the indispensablest beauty in knowing how to get done." Neither the historical nor the practical aspect of Fine Printing is lacking in fertility;

and whilst not assuming the *rôle* of possessor of the charming quality mentioned, the author is free to confess that his discrimination has been most taxed in the direction of "knowing how to get done"—to get done comprehensively, and to get done so that the work should not, in a pecuniary sense, be prohibitive.

In the Composition and Presswork chapters, the principles formulated are not from theoretical imaginings nor hearsay; but are principles that have stood the test of practice, and are the result of an effort to "prove all things," and to "hold fast that which is good." Order and system are important factors in the production of good work, and an endeavour has been made to emphasise their value. Beyond that, in essaying the erection of a sign-post to guide the compositor and the pressman, in some degree, in the way of higher and more meritorious work, both publishers and author have not been disregardful of the fact that "Example is better than Precept." It is not given to one, nor two, to acceptably expound all the bearings of so complex a subject as the practice of fine typography. That the compositor and the pressman may find the methods here advanced worthy consideration, the work in whose execution those methods have been used may not be esteemed an unsuitable guarantee.

G. J.

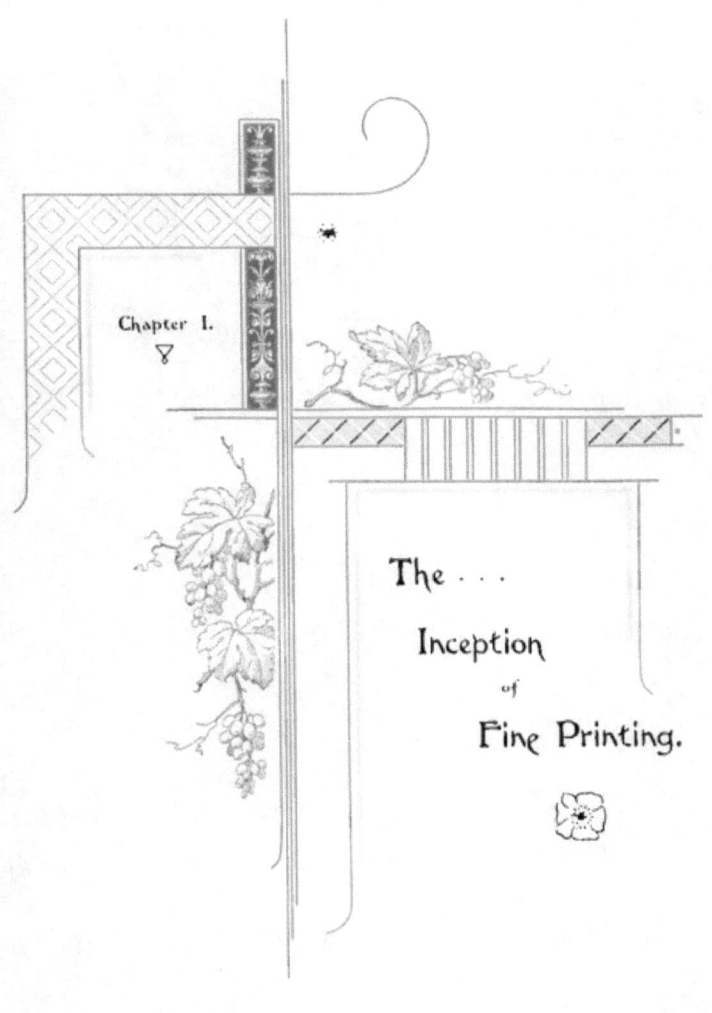

Chapter I.

The ...
Inception
of
Fine Printing.

FINE PRINTING.

CHAPTER I.

The Term "Fine Printing" America's due—The New World Pioneers of Fine Printing: Joseph A. Adams, James Glaestaeter, Oscar H. Harpel, William Jas. Kelly, William H. Bartholomew, Andreas Valette Haight, Samuel Reed Johnston, Theodore L. De Vinne, John F. Earhart—The Influence of German and Austrian Fine Printing—Some Notable Exponents: Büxenstein, Fasol, Albin M. Watzulik, Heinrich Knöfler and his Sons, Anton Halauska, Theodore Goebel—Progress in Kindred Arts: Type-founding, Manufacture of Printing Machinery, Ink-making, Paper-making, and Photo-Engraving.

THE terms "Artistic Printing" and "Fine Printing" are almost synonymous. Both have been brought into use to designate more particularly that section of the Job-work portion of the Art of Typography which has originated and developed so remarkably within the past thirty years; but the latter term has found more general acceptance of late years with best exponents of present day first-class printing in the United Kingdom, for more than one reason. Without being too pretentious to act discordantly with the reputed inherent modesty of good printers, the term "Fine Printing" comprehensively includes that Book and Magazine work which is not only a triumph of mechanical art, but which must, in the best sense of the word, be regarded as "fine."

And further, the term "Fine Printing," while being broader in conception, does not lend itself so freely to misapplication as that of "Artistic Printing." Alas! far too many are the examples sent broadcast, heedlessly branded "Artistic Printing," which not only do not possess any attribute approaching artistic merit, but do not show even an acquaintance with the elementary principles of typographic production.

To all lovers of good printing the law of cause and effect could provide no more striking exemplification—could afford no more interesting study—than is furnished in the comparatively recent progress of the "Art Preservative of all Arts."

It would be a matter of some conjecture to give the exact date when the causes resulting in the present high attainments of the art began to operate; but to America's sons undoubtedly belong the honour of having originated the movement which has made fine art printing in this country not only a possibility, but an actuality. And whether inventive type-founders, by the production of novel type faces and fanciful ornaments, stimulated American printers to endeavour to excel in their art, or whether enterprising printers made suggestions to and demands upon the type-founders that led to the development of the supply of material, is also a moot point. Certainly, many instances in subsequent years could be quoted to confirm the latter inference.

These matters, however, are of less moment than the consideration and recognition of the achievements of some of those pioneers who have done so much in raising the Art of Printing to its present high standard.

It was at a considerably earlier date than the year it has been thought well to give as covering, generally, the period of greatest interest in the advancement of fine job printing—with which this work is most nearly concerned—that Joseph A. Adams, the eminent New York engraver, demonstrated the excellence of hard packing and applied overlays for cuts in the production of "Harpers' Illustrated Bible."

It was before the year 1870, too, that James Glaestaeter (of the firm of Thitchner and Glaestaeter, of New York) had gained a reputation as a fine printer, and had been obliged to seek the assistance of the engraver in producing designs and tint blocks for his fancy job work, owing to the typographic resources of that period being more limited than Glaestaeter's ingenuity. He is credited with being the first letter-press printer to use tint blocks, and his tint work was distinguished for beautiful finish, brilliance, and evenness. He invented the Glaestaeter Distributor for machines like the Gordon press, with the disc system of distribution. In after years his invention was adapted by English machine manufacturers.

It was shortly before 1870, also, that Oscar H. Harpel, of Cincinnati, was engaged in producing his "Typograph; or, Book of Specimens." It is generally conceded that this work was the means of making more good printers than any other typographic handbook produced up to that time.

However, of the world's artist-printers William James Kelly must stand at the forefront. For the craft at large, fine job printing began when Kelly manipulated his first job and blended his first colours in the city of New York. "An army of ingenious, artistic followers have arisen; but none have ever equalled the master in design, in detail, or in the completeness of the whole creation, from type or rule to presswork. His work has always had a grace and loveliness peculiarly his own, which could only be inspired by a genius of the highest order."[*]

After demonstrating his talents in various parts of the United States, creating a renown probably unprecedented in the annals of typography, he went to the Paris Exposition of 1878, as representative exhibitor of American Printing. On his return to New York he associated himself in business with William H. Bartholomew, and in October, 1879, published

---

[*] A Study: By John Ransom.

the *American Model Printer*. This was the first technical journal of an artistic character introduced into this country, and to the few who were fortunate enough to secure copies it came as a revelation in typographic production; such luxuries in types and borders as displayed in its pages were unknown, and probably unthought of, in these isles. The cover of No. 3 — gold on solid black and in places on brilliant geranium-red, leaving a broad band and curve of white — remains to this day unsurpassed for effect and beauty of workmanship. The printing of gold on black or coloured ground, and being able to get the bronze to dust off clean, was a problem that took the uninitiated some considerable time to solve. However, it is now no secret that if the black or coloured ground be dusted over with magnesia before working the gold forme, no difficulty is experienced in cleaning off the superfluous bronze—provided it is not of too fine a quality—and the density of black or the brilliancy of colour is not greatly depreciated.

The *American Model Printer* proved to be in advance of the age, and its life was a brief one. As De Vinne wisely says, "True success is not the mere making of money, but the production of meritorious work." Regarded from this noble criterion, Kelly and Bartholomew attained the fullest measure of success, for they did grand pioneer work for the various admirable trade journals that have succeeded the *American Model Printer*.[*]

In the "Printers' International Specimen Exchange" of 1882 appeared another of Mr. Kelly's masterpieces—a representation of encaustic tile work surrounding a gold centre, the tiles being worked in three colours and two tints — showing to what perfection fine colour printing had been brought in America at that time.

---

[*] At a subsequent date, Mr. W. H. Bartholomew devoted himself to the production of half-tone pictures by his method of copper etching. Numerous examples of his work which show the highest degree of artistic excellence have appeared during recent years both in American and English trade journals.

Possibly, no name is more honoured amongst fine printers than that of Andreas Valette Haight. Prior to 1878, when he commenced in business on his own account at Poughkeepsie, on the Hudson, he had acquired a high reputation in the States for work characterised by a departure from delicate tints to more daring tones, and even brilliant dashes of full, rich colouring.

Mr. Haight's work is perhaps better known this side the Atlantic than that of the other great American job printers. A successful and progressive business enabled him to issue at different periods numerous collections of "Specimens of Printing," and these, through their wide circulation, have beyond question exercised a conspicuous influence in the advancement of modern artistic job work. In addition to these, in trade journals and exchanges, Mr. Haight has given the craft at large some notable examples of economy in working, by overlapping of tints and colours. One of these, a design in six workings, gave an actual effect of ten colours; and the title page to "Specimens of Printing, 1888," which was afterwards contributed to the "Printers' International Specimen Exchange," showed no less than ten tints and colours for three workings.

From the 1884 issue of "Specimens of Printing, by A. V. Haight," a billhead is selected for reproduction. It is not suggested that this is the original design from which the Ornamental Panel Style was evolved; but it is given rather as being thoroughly representative of a class of border arrangement that was extremely popular in this country at a little later period. That this particular job had considerable influence, however, is evidenced in the result of an open job competition in the autumn of 1884, when second honours were awarded for an example as near a copy in style of Haight's specimen as the competitor's slightly different material would permit!

Not the least important feature in a memorable career of faithful, persistent effort in stimulating job printers to "higher things" has been the designing by Mr. Haight of several excellent type faces and ornaments, the series of "Card Gothic" and "Atlanta" being those best known to British printers.

In 1875, the late Samuel Reed Johnston (chief of the printing department of the firm of Eichbaum and Co., Pittsburg, U.S.A.) produced the first examples of a system of typographic embellishment which he named "Owltype." The particular mode adopted in obtaining the plates for the production of the beautiful cloud-like, chaotic effects so well known in connection with this style of ornamentation, Johnston kept secret until the year 1887, when he divulged it to Mr. P. S. M. Munro, editor of the *American Art Printer*. Hence the various succeeding systems resulted from experiments instituted in order to produce similar typographic phenomena.

About 1883, John F. Earhart, then of Columbus, Ohio, patented his discovery under the title of "Chaostype." Subsequently, Anton Halauska, of Hallein-Salzburg, Austria, in emulating Earhart, obtained by pouring hot metal on damp metal a plate which, printed in gold and a colour over a brilliant red ground, gave a beautiful and striking effect; this he christened "Selenotype."

"Owltype," "Chaostype," and "Selenotype" have all had their disciples, and imitations of these systems for making job work effective were rife in Great Britain from about 1885 to 1890; but

> *Our little systems have their day,*
> *They have their day and cease to be.*

And in the fine printing of the present day this cloud-like decoration has no place.

To revert to Mr. Johnston. In 1887 he sent out a select collection of specimens containing several excellent practical exhibits of his invention, in bands and corners and other devices. Although original as a designer and colourist, and the successful exponent of a fine, pure style of type display, Johnston, singularly enough, always maintained the opinion that in becoming a printer he made a mistake, and that it was a calling for which he was not suited. The number who differ from that opinion exactly corresponds to the number who have had the opportunity of examining his work.

To be well versed in the history and traditions of the Art of Printing, to be thoroughly skilled in all branches of its technique, and to be a lucid writer on any of the various subjects connected with that art, is an array of accomplishments very seldom combined in an individual experience; yet in Theodore L. De Vinne, the chief of the well-known De Vinne Press, New York, is the embodiment of all these talents, and more.

The first is evidenced by two notable works from his facile pen—the "Invention of Printing," a volume of some five hundred pages, published in 1876, and "Historic Printing Types"; then, Mr. De Vinne's fame as a practical printer is world-wide; and next, his articles on technical subjects, from small matters of detail to questions of the highest import to Printing as an Art, have been published in every reputable trade journal in printerdom.

In the New World, at least, fine magazine and book printing and the name of Theodore L. De Vinne will ever be inseparable.

Within his experience has been the transition from wet paper to smooth polished dry paper for fine work; and he was amongst the first to perceive the advantages of the innovation. "It was found that cuts could be printed with a clearness not obtainable with wet paper; that for work needed in a hurry, to print by the dry process saved much time; and, moreover, it soon became apparent that dry printing on smooth paper was best." This is from Mr. De Vinne's own record of the change. Typographers who have had the pleasurable opportunity of examining the splendid work in the *Century* magazine—the best known in this country of the De Vinne Press publications—will readily admit the suitability of this smooth polished dry paper for bringing out the details of either woodcut or process block. The paper, however, is not the only agent necessary to the attainment of such perfection in fine printing, and Mr. De Vinne stated as recently as last year that it takes two or three days to accomplish the make-ready of a single forme of this magazine.

Many beautiful styles of type have been designed and promoted by the chief of the De Vinne Press. His *forte*, however, in the matter of type faces is generally and laudably in the direction of readableness. Hair-lines and excess of ornamentation evoke his satire. One of the most popular "faces" for job work in Great Britain to-day is the "De Vinne" series. Whether designed by Mr. De Vinne or only given his name in compliment, it is a very good indication of the class of type that finds his commendation—bold and clear enough to be easily, comfortably read, yet artistic withal. In proof of the appreciation of the "De Vinne" series it need only be mentioned that type-founders have produced the "face" in four degrees: square, condensed, extra condensed, and italic.

Few printing offices large or small can boast a stock of type which has been purchased on any plan that could be honoured with the title of "system." In most instances, unfortunately, it is the systematic element that is entirely lacking in the selection of type. "Here a little, there a little," would seem to be the general rule. Mr. De Vinne has shown more wisdom in this particular; and what is "believed to be the best arranged establishment in the world for every branch of typography" has been equipped with type selected on a well-defined principle—not at the caprice of the customer. The result is the distinctive style which has been so important a factor in making the firm famous.

Mr. De Vinne has many other admirable traits; but with these it is not within the province of this work to deal. As a leader in fine printing he stands pre-eminent, and possesses a reputation that has been won not only by taste and sound judgment, but by scrupulous care.

Of the many striking examples of American chromatic job work in the early volumes of the "Printers' International Specimen Exchange," none possess in greater degree the merit of artistic and telling effect than the contributions of John F. Earhart, then of Columbus, Ohio, U.S.A., now of Cincinnati. But even these, as well as his journal the *Superior Printer* splendid incentives though they were to the attainment of higher typographical excellence seem matters of small moment in the career of one who has given the printing fraternity of the globe so marvellous a work as the "Colour Printer."

Probably owing to its complex character and the requirement of profound knowledge gained from actual experience, colour printing is not a favourite subject with technical writers. Consequently, a work like Mr. Earhart's "Colour Printer," that is a most exhaustive practical treatise as well as a transcendent model of typographic art, is at once rare and useful.

It is not surprising that the work took many years—from before 1885 to 1892—to accomplish; for, besides engraving nearly the whole of the numerous diagrams, colour plates, and illustrations with his own hand, Mr. Earhart had his duties as chief of the growing business of Earhart and Richardson. Haste would have been a fatal element in a book representing some seven hundred workings! And the patience and analytical skill that enabled the author to obtain from twelve ordinary stock inks upwards of a thousand distinct gradations of colour and tint are as admirable as the great perseverance requisite to the carrying to a successful completion a treatise so comprehensive. Mr. Earhart's book contains ninety plates, some of which represent as many as eighteen workings, and the specially-designed initials and headpieces form in themselves miniature studies both in harmony and contrast.

Mr. Earhart's early productions entitle him to a prominent place as a pioneer of fine printing; but his genius as author and manipulator of the "Colour Printer" gives him a foremost position amongst the splendid galaxy of American artist-printers who followed Kelly's initiative.

The thought, intelligence, and perseverance of such of her sons as are here delineated, give to America the high distinction of having originated and extended the movement that has exercised so beneficial an influence on the typographers of the older nations of the world.

The value of that movement, if considered only in its relation to the commercial prosperity of the New World, it would be almost impossible to over-estimate; but, when it is regarded as having been the means of lifting the typographical craft of this country from the remarkable rut of inartistic sameness in which it had laboured for so many years and sending it along the high road towards grace and artistic perfection, then its value has an infinitely higher and nobler significance.

Several years before artistic job work had exponents in this country, both German and Austrian typographers had shown remarkable ability in the production of a class of fine job printing in character entirely different from the American work. While not possessing the new and striking qualities of the latter, it was notable for pure and delicate colouring, generally massive but exquisite arrangement of beautiful borders of Mediæval and Renaissance designs, and details of masterly finish.

In moulding the characteristic British fine printing of to-day, this German and Austrian work (which, being identical in style, can be accepted conjointly) has, in a different groove, exercised an influence almost equal in importance to that of the free and more graceful American productions. But to whom the credit of this high typographical influence is due is a somewhat difficult matter to divine. In the case of America, the tendency and importance of individual work are more easily identified; but as the original influence from the land of Gutenberg, Faust, and Schœffer was imparted to the printers of this

52, 54, 56, LONDON STREET, MAYFAIR.

Madam,

NOTWITHSTANDING that my intended alterations are not yet complete, the increased accommodation already gained has afforded very great advantage, both for the comfort of customers and the display of goods; I therefore beg to apprise you that in all Departments I am prepared to show the leading Novelties of the season.

I would call special attention to the following:

Dresses. Black Silks at old prices. French & Wool Poplins, French Beiges, Balernoes, Naples Cords, Silk Warps, Athol Lustrines, Wool Matelasses, Sateen Galateas, &c.

Lace and Hosiery. Ribbons and Gloves.

Household Linens. The leading makes in Irish, Barnsley, and Scotch Sheetings, Damask Cloths and Napkins, Huckabacks, &c. A large and varied stock of Nottingham Lace, Scotch Leno, and Muslin Long Curtains.

THE SHOW ROOMS
ARE REPLETE WITH EVERY NOVELTY IN

Mantles, Jackets, Paletots and Coats in the Newest Designs and Shapes. Dolmans, Visites, Military Coats and Fichus in Paris and London Styles at moderate cost. Children's Jackets in Coloured and Black Cloths.

Soliciting the favour of an early call,

I am, Madam,

Your obedient Servant,

JOSEPH LONG.

country mainly by the magnificent specimen sheets from the leading type-foundries, published in the *Printers' Register* in the year 1880 and subsequently, rather than by exchange of specimen books or work, hence the slight difficulty in awarding "honour to whom honour is due."

Certainly, such men as Wilhelm Büxenstein,* the artist-printer of Berlin, who died in 1886; the Brothers Grunert, also of Berlin, and Carl Fasol,† who died at Vienna in 1892, did much good service in the interests of German fine printing. But Herr Alexander Waldow,‡ in his biography of Albin M. Watzulik, the deaf and dumb foreman jobbing compositor of Pierer's Royal Printing Establishment (Geibel and Co.), in Altenburg, Saxony, gives a good general explanation of the way in which this influence was disseminated when he says: "At first there were a few especially gifted men, who distinguished themselves by their first-class original compositions, and sought to create works truly beautiful and excellent. These talented men became the teachers of the considerable number of jobbing compositors who now express themselves in works intended to satisfy the critical eye of the professional artist."

Herr Waldow claims for Watzulik that he "did for German job printing what Harpel did for America: he raised the standard of execution and set the style of design and display and colour that has prevailed almost ever since in the Fatherland."

After serving an apprenticeship rendered exceedingly arduous by his distressing affliction, Watzulik left his native town, Tyrnau, Hungary, in 1869, and became a news compositor in the "Leykam Josephsthal" Printing Establishment, at Graz. Twelve months later he accepted a

---

* Contributor to "International Specimen Exchange," 1883-88.

† Herr Carl Fasol was the inventor of "Stigmatype" printing, and a clever compositor; but his method, though artistic, was much too elaborate to be remunerative.

‡ Author of the "Cyclopædia of the Graphic Arts."

situation in the jobbing department, and within three months was promoted to first compositor. He left Graz in 1873 to take his situation at Altenburg.

Singularly enough, some of Herr Watzulik's work is particularly "un-German-like" in style, especially in the treatment of brass rule, which he manipulates into scrolls, fans, flowers, and other devices with the facility and precision of an adept. As Herr Waldow says, his work "is remarkable for freshness of style and inventiveness in design; and whether dealing with handsome title-pages for type-founders' specimen books, business cards, or circulars, the taste of the true artist and colourist, and the practised skill of the master-craftsman are visible in every detail of the work that comes from his hands.

"It has been said that Watzulik's genius lay only in one direction, so often found in American work, only seeking to arouse the attention of beholders by quaint figures, being fond of using rule designs in fantastical forms. That this is an erroneous opinion those who have had the opportunity of seeing any number of his productions will at once admit, as they invariably accord with the purest artistic taste, and yet show decided genius and versatility. Then, how beautifully he executes all his designs; composition and colouring are so rendered as to produce the most exquisite typographical effects; every piece of border, every ornament, every line of type seeming as though it had been specially cut for the space it occupies and would fit nowhere else. The quaint designs which play such an important part in his work require a large amount of technical ability, as well as an unlimited acquaintance with all the appliances at his command."

Then, at Vienna, in 1869, Heinrich Knöfler began to produce some of those wonderful masterpieces which have made his name justly famous as the finest colour printer and engraver the world has ever known. As is generally understood, Knöfler's work consisted of the production of religious subjects from marvellously delicate woodcuts of his own execution, and incomparably printed on the hand-press by himself, with inks of his own mixing and grinding.

The work of art, by any process, that surpasses Knöfler's in purity and brilliancy of colouring and truth of delineation has yet to be produced ; and a writer has well said that Knöfler's productions, "whether looked upon artistically or from the printer's standpoint, are beyond all praise."

Subscribers to the *British Printer* were favoured with an excellent example of one of Knöfler's smaller masterpieces, in No. 8 of that journal, in the reproduction, by his sons, Heinrich and Rudolph, of the portrait of Johann Rudolph Kutschker, the first Bishop of Vienna. And at the International Exhibition of Fine Letterpress Printing held in the Stationers' Hall, London, in October, 1889, a splendid collection of Knöfler prints was on show. What true printer could regard these gems of chromo-xylography without experiencing a deepening of his esteem for a craft that presents such extraordinary possibilities?

Without doubt, Knöfler's work was exceptional in character—the demand, too, for such work was exceptional—but his genius was more than exceptional, it was wonderful. The oft-quoted illustration of the celebrated painter who, when asked what he mixed with his paints to obtain such beautiful effects, answered "Brains," is too insignificant a summary to a consideration of Knöfler's qualities, for "soul" is more evident in his work than any other principle.

In Anton Halauska, of Hallein-Salzburg, Austrian fine printing has had a most able exponent. When his father (who had formerly been printer to the Imperial University) re-established himself at Waidhofen, on the Ybbs, in 1869, young Halauska was inducted into the "mysteries" of the art of typography. Before 1871, "his tastes led him to prefer the more ornamental walks of the profession, and he had developed a strong natural ability for 'decorative' and colour printing. Some of his specimens produced at this period evince an ability highly creditable."*

As already related in this work, Herr Halauska discovered the system of embellishment named "Selenotype," for this he received a gold medal at the Linz Exhibition; and, in recognition of his efforts to improve the Art of Printing, the Austrian Government bestowed upon him the exceptional honour of permission to use the imperial eagle as his business sign.

Furthermore, German graphic art has received valuable assistance and elucidation in the literary work of the gifted Theodore Goebel, formerly editor of the *Journal für Buchdruckerkunst*. Herr Goebel was editor of the *Journal* from 1871 to 1878, resigning then only in order that he might make more independent use of his wide practical experience, and thus render still better service to the leading literature of the art.

An English translation of an article which appeared in the *Journal* for March, 1893, and of which Herr Goebel was the subject, contained the following acknowledgment of his genius. "By his thorough knowledge in all the departments of the typographic art—knowledge gained, not by a dry study of books, but by practical experience—by his untiring zeal in collecting everything that was new and was worth knowing, by his keen insight, and not least by the brilliancy and clearness of his composition, he not only raised the *Journal* to the height which its founder[1] had always had in view, but enlarged its scope and interests principally by means of his extensive foreign relations."‡ It is worthy of note, in passing, that it was during Herr Goebel's editorship German text was discarded in favour of Roman type for the literary portion of the *Journal*.

The renowned second volume of " Wiens Buchdrucker-Geschichte," § by Anton Meyer, from the press of Herr Friedrich Jasper, containing

* *British Printer*, No. 4, 1888. † Dr. H. Meyer.
‡ *British Printer*, No. 33, 1893. § " History of Printing in Vienna."

twenty-five artistic supplements produced by various printers of Vienna, is also a remarkable instance of the high excellence of the printing art in Austria.

The achievements of such geniuses as these give the clue to the superiority of German and Austrian typography over that of the other European nations at a comparatively early date. Not that British printers were lacking the ability to do fine work, as subsequent events have conclusively proved; but their latent talents needed stimulation, and with that stimulation the advantage of the superior facilities possessed by the printers of America and Germany. Given these, British job-work typographers quickly demonstrated that not only were they capable of executing work equal in merit to that of their American or German *confrères*, but inventive enough to create a style which cannot be considered other than the "happy medium" between the styles of the two nations who inspired them to emulation.

Indeed, at the present time evidence is plentiful that the modern English style of job work is in turn exercising considerable influence on German typographers, even to the extent of a more artistic and less conventional use of their own material. A perusal of the advertisement pages of Schelter and Giesecke's *Typographische Mitteilungen* for 1892 or 1893, Julius Mäser's *Typographische Jahrbücher* for 1894, and other modern German productions will disclose semi and three-quarter borders, the use of pictorial vignettes, border bands intersected with wording, and even grouping display. Neither is evidence wanting that British fine job work is now being accepted by other nations as a model to be followed.

On the question of initiative, as between printer and type-founder, enough has already been said; but of course the forward movement in fine typography could only have been rendered generally practicable by a corresponding advance in the leading auxiliary arts, such as type-founding, the manufacture of printing machinery, and inks, and papers.

British type-founders apparently regarded the inception of fine printing as a "nine days' wonder," rather than as an important sign of modern artistic progress and a movement not only "come to stay" but destined to develope in a remarkable manner. Thus, for several years the leading American and German founders had a clear field for the introduction of their beautiful and unique productions. And having overcome that—in this case slight—obstacle, the inherent prejudice said to be characteristic of "Britishers" in regard to accepting new methods, they did not fail to make the fullest use of the opportunity.

By the year 1870, hand-presses had already been superseded, to a great extent, by cylinder and platen machines for job work. From time to time as constant progress necessitated, inventive genius extended the capabilities and improved the qualities of these machines until the requisite strength and rigidity were gained. Then the handicraft of the printer's engineer only needed supplementing by the skill of the artist-pressman. When the latter discarded woollen and indiarubber blankets for the sheets of paper and cardboard arrangement technically known as "hard packing," he undoubtedly applied the keystone to the fabric of fine printing; for without fine presswork the beauties of the type-founder's art, and in turn the compositor's talent, would be entirely lost.

When fine printing began, the stock list of the ink-maker did not comprise much beyond black and primary and secondary colours. Gradations of colour and tints the art printer had to obtain by mixing and reducing to suit his particular requirements. As art typography gradually extended its influence, however, ink-makers with commendable enterprise greatly improved the quality of their products, and by degrees increased the range so that it now includes colours and tints of almost every conceivable hue.

And paper-makers, with the aid of modern machinery and ingenious devices for sizing, calendering, and embossing, have been enabled to produce papers of considerable variety and suitable in substance and finish for high-class printing. Of these, the most favoured received the appellation of "art paper," and is now a general product with most makers of note. Besides white and toned, it is made in a variety of choice tints, has a fine appearance, is practically of same surface both sides; and, what is more important still, is calculated to bring out the full beauties of woodcut, process block, type, and ink.

Another important modern development germane to fine printing is the art of Photo-Engraving, or reproduction by process, which, despite the deprecation of the wood engraver and Professor Herkomer, R.A., has made great progress and found general appreciation in recent years. If it be true that "Process is substituted for Art," how can Alma-Tadema's dictum, "that Art has to awaken in the spectator a higher sense of the beautiful," be applied in this case? Surely, that "higher sense of the beautiful" is more fully attained by work absolutely faithful in representation and possessing a fineness of detail far beyond the skill of hand engraving, than by a style of presentment oftentimes crude in execution, and occasionally marred by the vagaries of the delineator! All wood engravers are not Knöflers.

To the lay mind, therefore, it is no matter for surprise that "process" obtains, and obtains increasingly; rather would it be remarkable if so important an invention failed in its mission to further the interests of Art. Then, apart from holding "the mirror up to Nature" more appreciably, process-engraving gives several advantages, among others being the reduction or enlargement of the subject to suit particular needs. All printers are not successful in obtaining artistic results from process work, it is true; but failure is more often due to ignorance of treatment, or unsuitability of paper, than to fault of the system.

The importance of photo-engraving in its relation to the art of fine printing is such as to command due consideration, Professor Herkomer's aversion notwithstanding.

Thus by a happy combination of general progress in kindred arts and the "meritorious work" of some of the craft's truest geniuses, within the past twenty-five years has been brought about one of the most extraordinary developments in the Art of Printing since its invention by Gutenberg some four hundred and forty years ago, at Mentz, where he,

> . . . . . *with toil incessant, wrought*
> *The imitative lines of written thought,*

with the first movable types and a wooden press!

In 1891, British typographical authorities considered that the "Art Preservative of Arts" was fast becoming a Fine Art. Since that time progress has not flagged; therefore, if then it was regarded as imminent, may it not, in 1895, be safely accepted as *un fait accompli?*

ALDWORTH, SUSSEX.

WOOD ENGRAVING.

And one, an English home — gray twilight poured
  On dewy pastures, dewy trees,
  Softer than sleep; all things in order stored,
A haunt of ancient Peace. — TENNYSON.

Chapter II.

Fine Printing
in the
United Kingdom.

Its Commencement
and Progress.

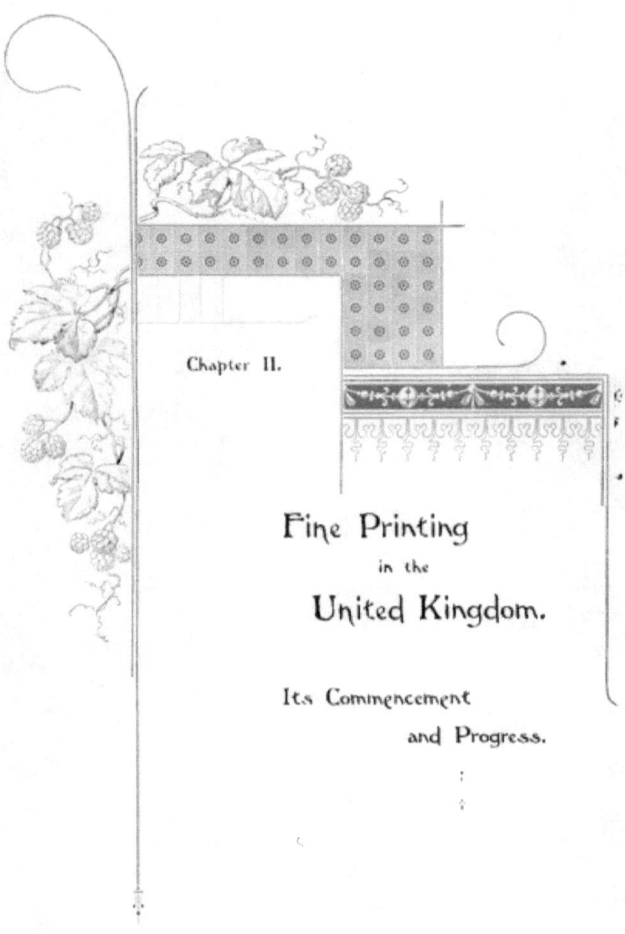

CHAPTER II.

The state of British Job Work in 1877 and 1878—"Painful plainness"—The first Agency for supplying American material—The Inauguration of the "Printers' International Specimen Exchange": Its value to the Craft—*Hailing's Circular:* the pioneer of British artistic printing journalism—The introduction of German Borders, etc.—An extraordinary job—A model Type-founder's Specimen Book—The *Modern Printer* and its work—"Too much of a good thing!"—The *American Art Printer*—The *British Printer*—George W. Jones institutes a New Style of Fine Work: "Something New in Letterpress Printing"—Vignettes in Job Work—Uniformity in Display—Growth and success of the *British Printer*—The International Exhibition of Fine Printing—"Grouping Style": Its unique value in Fine Printing—"Geometrical Arrangement" of Rule and Border—The possibilities of the Art—The importance of the Development.

FROM the time when Caxton issued the quaint advertisement of the "good chepe" Romish service books used at "Salisburi," down to 1877, when Thomas Hailing, of Cheltenham, sent out the first number of his famous *Circular*, the progress of job printing in Great Britain had been somewhat tardy, and the innovations denoting advancement, artistically, comparatively few. It is true that occasionally the old printers would produce jobs of exceptional merit, and home type-founders introduce an ornamental combination, or a border, or a type face possessing artistic qualities; but these were not followed up with any remarkable degree of typographical enthusiasm, nor did they eventuate in any notable development of the art. Neither does the year 1877 furnish any particularly striking indications of artistic development in the job work of this country. The date, nevertheless, has some claim to notice ; for in addition to being the year of the Caxton Exhibition, it was the year in which the idea of a Specimen Exchange—a subject that had already received considerable attention in American trade journals—was first suggested to British printers. And the fact of the issuance of *Hailing's Circular* at this period with a view to " educating the public in some of the mysteries of printing," and in the hope that knowledge would " break down the barriers of jealous exclusiveness" that divided trade from trade, profession from profession, as well as to exert an influence in encouraging good work, is an indication that the author at least appreciated the desirability of cultivating—in place of the long-fostered, suspicious reserve with which old-time printers guarded their methods—a spirit more in accordance with an age of intelligence and progress.

But, though in 1877 there were signs of a typographical awakening, and influences were being generated which in course of time produced good results, the absolute fairness of the following estimation of British job work by a distinguished American printer, written shortly after his return from a visit to Europe in 1878, cannot be gainsaid :

> The general peculiarity of English job printing is its abruptness and sameness of appearance—with nothing to charm the eye or enrapture the sense. Notwithstanding this, there is a character, and that is its painful plainness, lacking nearly all the requisites pertaining to Art.

Thus, at the end of 1878 there was still not much of the artistic element in British job printing. At the same time, while admitting that " painful plainness " was the leading characteristic of the productions of home printers prior to the elevating influence of American and German typography and the introduction of more artistic facilities, there is no lack of evidence that really good printing, praiseworthy alike in composition and presswork, was by no means rare in this country.

The reproduction in this work of an 1877 circular is a verification of the truth of this statement. Though clean in appearance, well displayed and properly spaced, the finish of details all that could be desired—manifesting an acquaintance with the principles that underlie the highest typographic production—yet it is not more than an average example of the work produced by many printers in Great Britain at that period. Rather plain, it is true; but this indicates dearth of artistic material more than the want of artistic taste. In passing, it may be mentioned that the reprint surpasses the original in one particular only, that of paper.

Coming to the year 1879, however, the combined influences that started the revolutionising of British job printing become apparent.

Obviously, next to the skill of the manipulator comes the material with which he obtains pleasing results. The foremost in importance of these influences, therefore, was the establishing of an agency for supplying the productions of the American type-foundries.

Towards the end of 1878, Mr. M. P. McCoy, after superintending a most interesting and practical exhibit of American type and machinery at the Paris Exposition, took up a commission to import the productions of Messrs. MacKellar, Smiths, and Jordan, of Philadelphia, and came to this country. But not until 1879, when Mr. McCoy joined the firm of Messrs. J. L. Chaplin and Co., then of Rathbone Place, London, who subsequently issued the "Specimen Sheet of New Impressions" (12 pp. imperial quarto), can it be said that American type and material were brought generally before the notice of British printers.

Within a year or two of this date that firm was operating the productions of some eight or ten Transatlantic type-foundries, in addition to the supplying of American machinery and other appliances; and enterprising home printers were soon enabled to become acquainted with, among others, the charm and novelty—so long unknown quantities in the printing offices of this country—of the "Chinese," "Japanese,"

"Egyptian," and "Zigzag" combination borders, as well as the "Cabalistic," "Filigree,"* "Campanile," and "Radiant" type faces, and many ornaments. Besides novelty, the American borders possessed another admirable feature. The various pieces being cast on the point system, the ease with which they could be justified with pica and its multiples was as astonishing as it was pleasing.

In its early days the venture had its trials. The "insular prejudices" of Britishers have already been alluded to, and those were not wanting who declared that British printers had ample facilities of home manufacture. Probably it was natural to resent competition from abroad, even though it was from "our kin beyond the sea"; but it must be admitted there was little of the progressive spirit in the resentment. The early printers realised to a very limited extent the future greatness of the art they promoted. Similarly, the importance of this innovation to the development of Fine Printing was very faintly perceived; still, a grain or two of the noble-mindedness that characterised the determination of the great Italian printer, Aldus Pius Manutius, " to be useful to men," to "labour continuously," and to "endeavour to make constant progress," would at least have been preferable. "Progress" should be the watchword in every sphere of labour, and pre-eminently in that of the "Art Preservative."

The slight drawbacks aside, however, there was very little hindrance to the acceptance of American printing material, and within a comparatively short period there was a strong desire in many quarters for artistic and striking effects in letterpress printing, created in great measure by the accounts in English trade journals of the high achievements of American craftsmen.

Then in 1879, after being in abeyance for two years owing to differences of opinion as to the method of control, Mr. Thomas Hailing

---

* Imported by Messrs. Caslon and Co., of London, in 1879.

propounded a scheme that enabled Mr. Andrew W. Tuer, editor of the *Paper & Printing Trades Journal*, to successfully inaugurate the "Printers' International Specimen Exchange."

To the first volume, issued in 1880, there were one hundred and seventy-eight contributors; but so successful was this movement for the interchange of handiwork and the raising of the standard of excellence in the art that the number rapidly advanced to three hundred and fifty, then to three hundred and seventy-five, and later to four hundred.

Of this institution it would be impossible to express too high an opinion. From the date of the first volume down to the present day it has, year after year, always been the faithful index of this country's typographical progress and development. In addition to this, the many contributions from foreign typographers have greatly enhanced its value, rendering it at once unique in interest and technical worth.

Occasionally typographical critics and some of the more skilful contributing members have thought that the matter of rejecting somewhat indifferent specimens might have been dealt with more drastically. There is no doubt that every volume has had its percentage of inferior examples; but though the exclusion of these would have ensured a more perfect collection, the difficulties of those in the position of "more responsibility and less freedom" would have been materially increased; and one of the best objects, namely, the raising the standard of execution, would to a great extent have been defeated. The extremely nice discrimination required in this connection is apparent when it is considered that the most humble of those seeking acceptance had at least the desire to improve; and how could this obtain better effect than by association with their more gifted *confrères*? Again, is there one amongst the craft's highest geniuses who has not learned something even from examples of "how *not* to do it"?

As to its value as a technical educator the "Printers' International Specimen Exchange" needs no demonstration; like the sunshine, it "is its own witness." From so large a fund of object lessons in the art the studious craftsman can at all times find something for his edification. Of all the good influences in circulation of late years for the elevation of the job printer, probably none has been more fruitful in good results than the "Exchange." To not a few of the foremost fine printers of the present age the date of connection with it indicates that "tide" in their affairs, which, although it may not have led "on to fortune," has culminated in their success as exponents of fine art printing—a consummation more to be desired than "the mere making of money"; and it is not too much to say that it has created a feeling of kindly interest between the craftsmen of the different nations represented.

All honour, then, to those whose exertions were instrumental in inaugurating and carrying to successful issue so excellent an institution as the "Printers' International Specimen Exchange." To each, individually, it may well be said:

> *Not only has our art by thee been raised,*
> *But thou hast caused us in ourselves more pride*
> *To take, our craftsmen more respected are,*
> *And all our daily work is dignified.*
>
> HILTON TESTIMONIAL.

It was also in 1879 that *Hailing's Circular*—having received as hearty a reception from the craft as from the public, whom alone it was originally intended to enlighten—developed into a trade journal of considerable artistic merit, having regard to the facilities available in this country at that period. Issued at first as a four-page quarto type specimen sheet with an introduction, Mr. Hailing now increased it to double that number of pages, adding original and technical literature of a highly interesting nature.

The following year the *Circular* was again increased, this time to twelve pages, and Mr. William Hailing (the author's brother) took up the editorial duties. The journal continued its most useful career for several years, appearing from time to time up to within some five years

ORNAMENTAL PANEL STYLE.

Specimens of Printing
by A. V. Haight.
1884

ago, when its publication—which had always been a labour of love—was rendered to some extent unnecessary by the success of other high-class trade journals in whose production were employed the indispensable adjuncts of fine typography: modern material and appliances. *Hailing's Circular* accomplished valuable pioneer work in British artistic printing journalism, and its charm of phraseology has never been surpassed. Bear with just one example in the following short extract from an editorial on "Do your Best:"*

> The strength of a chain is no greater than that of its weakest link. So again we say, Press on! Even if failure stares you in the face. Better attempt and fail than not attempt at all. But failure seldom comes to the honest worker. Therefore, do not be discouraged. If you believe a piece of your work will be improved by a little more painstaking, hesitate not to give it. By all means never let any pass out of your hands that you *know* to be imperfect. And then work will gradually become to you what the Designer no doubt intended it to be, your greatest and most unalloyed blessing.

The noble aim of the author of the *Circular* was to "raise the status of printers and printing generally," and how thoroughly that aim was realised is evidenced in the fact that he is universally regarded as the "Father of British fine printing."

In addition to the services to the art already cited, Mr. Hailing issued two specimen books of work produced in his office, the first appearing in 1880. The collection evoked the highest encomiums of the best judges of typographical excellence at that period, and was introduced in the following characteristic diction:

> The true artist is most keenly alive to his own shortcomings, and can gauge his abilities at something like their worth. That which you here find worthy of following, follow; what you deem unworthy, pass by; or, better still, improve upon. This volume I liken to a simple stone, which may be used in the construction of a vast bridge across the stream of Mediocrity. Where are the labourers who will add the remaining stones to complete the bridge?

---

* No. 6: Summer, 1880.

Succeeding years have proved this specimen book was more than a "simple stone" in the noble structure of fine printing—indeed, nothing less than a foundation stone "well and truly laid."

The productions of American type-founders were not destined to long hold the undivided patronage of British printers, and the prelude to the enterprise of German type-founders was a two-page octavo specimen sheet of Herr Otto Weisert's "Ronde" script. This was published in the *Printers' Register* of November, 1879; but the fact is noteworthy only as being preliminary, and not from anything remarkable in this particular type. But coming to the same month of the following year, 1880, when the specimen sheet of the beautiful "Florentine" border from the foundry of Messrs. Schelter and Giesecke, of Leipzig, was issued through the same journal, a period of considerably greater moment to the development of British fine printing is reached.

The border in question was of a class entirely different from any that had formerly been placed before home printers. As the name indicates, it was representative of the graceful Italian school of design; but one of the most notable features was the great number of characters—seventy-eight with solid ground and a like number with stippled ground—ranging in size from an en up to five ems cicero, with gable ornaments, medallions and capitals. The portion of the sheet illustrating its use was of masterly execution, of that perfect symmetricalness which distinguishes the typography of the Fatherland, and was much enhanced by the free use of portions of the no less beautiful "Grecian" border by the same founders.

It is not matter for great surprise, however, that British work gave very little indication of this new influence for some two or three years: the difficulty of obtaining the correct architectural effect without mitred divisional rules, the quads and spaces necessary for the justification of a body unknown in English printerdom, and the price of so multifarious a combination, mainly accounting for this. Here and there jobs appeared with portions of these borders, a page in *Hailing's Circular* in 1881, and some half-dozen small examples in the "Specimen Exchange" of 1882, to wit; but it was not until the Printing Exhibition in 1883, in Mr. W. J. Sanger's first prize specimen of artistic printing, that an array of German material was displayed in any individual British job. This truly remarkable specimen—which entailed no less than fifty-three workings—was essentially German in style, and in addition to Schelter and Giesecke's "Grecian" border and other ornaments, contained a handsome four-colour border from the foundry of Otto Weisert, at Stuttgart.

In passing, it may be noted that the critical interest evoked by Mr. Sanger's extraordinary specimen was not unproductive of good; and apart from the true British perseverance evinced in the successful carrying out of a job of fifty-three workings—an accomplishment which stands, and probably will long remain, unrivalled—it was by far the most artistic and meritorious of any British job produced up to that year.

To return to the subject of German borders. Having passed the crucial test, from 1883 to the present day there has been no limit to the supply of beautiful and useful material from Continental type-founders. In due course appeared Schelter and Giesecke's "Akanthea," consisting of one hundred and ninety-four pieces, with one section for two colours; "Holbein," with suitable outer ornaments, over a hundred pieces, one of the most favoured borders in this country; and the beautiful two-colour Gothic initials, in four sizes, with appropriate filigree ornamentation; Bauer and Co.'s handsome "Heraldic" border; Otto Weisert's three-colour Roman initials; labour-saving divisional brass rule of all degrees and mitres; together with many other aids to the production of fine printing, the bare enumeration of which would extend this chapter to an undue length.

It is well within the mark to say that Messrs. Schelter and Giesecke's enterprise has been highly beneficial to British fine printing. The specimen book of their productions, issued in the year 1886, 360 pp. imperial octavo (supplemented later by 150 pp.) is one of the finest and completest of its class ever produced. Until the publication of the specimen book—compiled in a similar way—of the Woellmer Foundry, Berlin, last year, Schelter and Giesecke's book was unrivalled. The title pages to the various sections of material are all masterpieces of the typographic art: composition and presswork are as near perfection as it is possible to attain, and each is a distinct study in rich, harmonious colouring.

The publication of the *Modern Printer*, in March, 1884, marks the date of commencement of a British trade journal solely devoted to the advancement of artistic typography. Its advent was most opportune. The *American Model Printer*, during the preceding four years, had excited the admiration of some few British printers; but the elaborate masterpieces exhibited in that beautiful journal, though eminently suggestive to the more accomplished Transatlantic craftsman, presented to the mind of the average printer of this country ideals altogether beyond his reach, and commercially prohibitive withal. Thus, in aiming at the "gradual cultivation by easy stages of the latent talents of the English printer," the promoters of the *Modern Printer* recognised the need of the period.

Although the *Modern Printer* did not live to see "English printing in the front rank among the nations," during the two years of its existence it rendered most valuable help in that direction by articles elucidating modern appliances and methods, by examples at once artistic and thoroughly practicable, and by instituting job competitions for the encouragement and development of native talent.

Under the conductorship of Mr. M. P. McCoy, whose experience had been mostly of a Transatlantic character, the style and influence of the *Modern Printer* were, naturally, distinctly *à l'Americain*.

During the early part of its career the MacKellar, Smiths, and Jordan's "Arboret" combination border was brought out. Of all the excellent American borders none equalled this in popularity. Whether or not it surpassed in intrinsic beauty the "Silhouette," which appeared in the autumn of 1882, only involves a point of taste, and "tastes differ," as everyone knows. The "Arboret" had the advantage of appealing to a *clientèle* whose artistic faculties had been heightened by upwards of two years of typographical progress; and herein, in all probability, lies the cause of its greater success.

To such a degree, however, did the series of "Arboret" border affect the style of British job printing for some few years that those who regarded the art's highest welfare advised a more discreet use. The counsel was timely, and more than justified by the result: the beginning of a new style of art printing that, in its full development, is neither American nor German, but essentially British.

To compare the relative importance of American and German typographical influences on British work would be cultivating invidiousness. Such a consummation, it is almost superfluous to say, is entirely foreign to the purpose of this work. Suffice it to record that in moulding the distinctive character of this country's present style the one has been the necessary concomitant of the other; neither dispensable, both essential. For in the early stages of its development, at least, British fine printing owed its chief charm to American types and German borders.

In the matter of supplying material, both American and German founders have shown no lack of enterprise, the former country being most conspicuously represented in the productions of MacKellar, Smiths, and Jordan, of Philadelphia; and the latter in those of Schelter and Giesecke, of Leipzig.

To return to the narrative. Ere the valedictory number of the *Modern Printer*[*] had reached the craft, two new art printing journals — both destined to affect the typography of this country, one in a pre-

---

[*] No. 3 of Vol. II. was published in December, 1885; the completing quarterly number of this, the last, volume did not appear until August, 1888.

eminent degree had been inaugurated in order that technically there should more "lyght be": the *American Art Printer* in January, 1887, and the *British Printer* in the same month of 1888; the former being published by Mr. C. E. Bartholomew, of New York, with Mr. P. S. M. Munro, an artist-printer and journalist of high repute, as editor; and the latter being founded by Mr. Robert Hilton, in conjunction with Mr. G. W. Jones, and printed at the office of Messrs. Raithby and Lawrence, of Leicester.

The *American Art Printer* was similar in size and style to its predecessor the *American Model Printer*, and essayed the exposition of the advanced culture of the printing art. To say that this lofty ideal was not only attained but sustained and developed, is bare acknowledgment of great achievements in fine printing. Naturally, its efficacy was greatest amongst the craft of the United States; at the same time, it was instrumental in guiding those British printers who came under its influence into a purer and more chaste style of typography. The examples of process engraving, too—a class of illustration largely affected by this journal on its transition from a two-monthly to a monthly issue, in 1892—were unsurpassed, if not unsurpassable, in delicacy of detail and artistic finish. Although the art of fine printing in the United States is not likely to decline in consequence of the recent discontinuance of the *American Art Printer* while it has such able exponents as the *Inland Printer* (Chicago), *Paper and Press* (Philadelphia), the *Artist Printer* (St. Louis), and the *Engraver and Printer* (Boston), still that discontinuance involved a great loss to all appreciators of fine art work.

But the *British Printer* more closely concerns the subject of this chapter. Coincidently with the *American Art Printer*, it was founded on the lines of a predecessor, the size and literary arrangement being similar to the *Modern Printer*. In addition, however, to being a two-monthly instead of a quarterly journal, the *British Printer* possessed another advantage over its prototype, in that American, German, and English material were brought into combination in its production.

British job printing, like all other developments, has had its phases. Following the introduction of American types and borders, it was characterised by a liberal display of these excellent aids to art: oftentimes used, it must be admitted, "not wisely, but too well." The same remark as fittingly applies to the early use of German borders, which were instrumental in bringing about the next noticeable change in style. Subsequently, the character of British work alternated, some jobs having a strong tendency towards American typography, while others were quite German-like in the massive arrangement of borders. In due course this led up to a style that is perhaps best described as "Americo-German" a combination of the productions of type-founders of both countries and "Americo-German" was the predominating style of the early numbers of the *British Printer.*

In order to consider the next important influence in the development of home job typography it is necessary to leave, for a brief period, the career of the *British Printer.*

Ere the second number of that journal was issued to the craft Mr. George W. Jones, who had been mainly responsible for its typography, accepted an overseership at the Darien Press, Edinburgh. Mr. Jones's work at Leicester had always been characterised by chasteness and finish; but the "invigorating air of the north seems to have had a refreshing effect" on his typographical faculties, for he soon "developed a new style of display, in which rules and simple line ornaments" were "gracefully combined."* This new style is a point of more than passing interest in connection with the subject of British fine printing, inasmuch as it indicates the period when the art assumed a more distinctive character and entered upon that course of development which has placed it in the "front rank among the nations" and given it some claim to be regarded as a fine art.

* *British Printer,* No. 4, July-August, 1888.

So that effect may be given to the significance of this new style it has been deemed advisable to reproduce two typical examples in illustration of its tendency. They have been selected from a book of specimens, entitled "Something New in Letterpress Printing," issued by Mr. Jones from the Darien Press early in 1889.

Some six months later—January-February, 1889—the *British Printer* again referred to the "wonderfully taking new style of design" that Mr. Jones had inaugurated, and assisted its promotion by giving examples.

> Graceful type and ornamental combinations and dainty tinting rival each other in admirable effects. There is no very elaborate composition in any of these specimens; ornament is used sparingly, but every bit tells, and as a rule the whole of any job is almost entirely in one tint, with just an initial, a rule, a small emblem or arms in another and more decided colour. Some of the tints are difficult to describe, thus fulfilling Ruskin's definition of a true art colour. The new pictorial vignettes are used in a novel style that will find many imitators as soon as they are seen. Another feature is that in the majority of these specimens only two or three faces of type—sometimes only one—are used, yet in every case the effect is good.

The use of vignettes in job work found favour with British printers in 1887, when Messrs. Zeese and Co., of Chicago, introduced a series of small pictorial electros. This was supplemented, in 1888, by a number of sea, river, and pastoral views, intended chiefly for use in corners, imported by Mr. Frederic Wesselhoeft, and these are the vignettes alluded to in the foregoing criticism.

In "Something New in Letterpress Printing," vignettes were used to good purpose. In some instances they were printed in delicate tints, the artistic appearance of the job being enhanced thereby, without in any way detracting from the value of the announcement—nay, rather was it rendered more arrestive. But the most remarkable feature of this collection was the artistic simplicity of the composition, which exhibited a far more correct appreciation of the legitimate use of ornament than had hitherto been demonstrated. "No very elaborate composition; ornament is used sparingly." For years more than one good printer

Offizieller Katalog
und
Führer
durch die
Industrie-Ausstellung
zu
Neustadt 1887.

Herausgegeben
unter Kontrolle des Ausstellungskomitees
von
Dr. Heinrich Stamm.

Gedruckt von
Julius Emil Haisburger
1887

Preis 1 Mark.

had sternly declined to give way to the innovation of fancy printing owing to its over-elaborateness and superfluity of ornament. This new style opened up the avenue to the popularisation of fine work. Here was truly artistic typography without intricacy in composition; ornament and vignette brought into use, and yet the most stringent law of the old school, that printed matter exists for the type display and not for the ornament, duly observed.

It is well known that some ten or twelve years ago it was a rule to make display matter—with a few exceptions, book titles chiefly—as diversified as possible. The productions of the type-founder favoured that style, well-graded series of a design, except in plain type or blacks, being very rare. Displaying jobs in uniformity—that is, using not more than two or three faces of type similar in character, or several sizes of a series—seems to be of American origin, but for home printers the style had already received exposition from Mr. Jones in several examples in Messrs. Raithby and Lawrence's Specimen Book of 1887. In "Something New," uniformity constituted the ruling principle of the type display. Add to the points already cited as distinguishing this collection the adoption of a judicious method in jobs of two or more workings by which intricate make-up was avoided, and some of the best features of modern British fine work are clearly perceptible.

The influx of labour-saving material since 1888 has made diversity easily achievable; two other capital systems of display have also been evolved and rendered definable; but to George W. Jones must be awarded the credit of instituting the fundamental principles that, judiciously fostered, gave to British fine work its distinctive qualities.

Now to return to the subject of the *British Printer*. Happily for fine printing, Mr. Jones's successor at Leicester, Mr. Robert Grayson, was pre-eminently "the right man in the right place." British fine work had just entered upon what has proved to be the most important phase of its development. The production of high-class work at this time was by no means extensive. Excellent work was being done in some few well-known houses; but the influences operating to higher attainments in the art were not widespread, and the task of practical demonstration, necessary to a general acceptance by the craft of a more artistic system of typography, devolved upon the new journal. To this work of dissemination the genius represented by the *British Printer* was most unsparingly applied. Mr. Hilton's vigorous editorship was ably supported by Mr. Grayson's typographical skill; and accepting and working upon the inexorable principle, that "such as would excel in Art must excel in Industry," progress was natural.

A lengthy diatribe on the phenomenal growth and success of the *British Printer* would be superfluous in view of the fact that its position as the foremost exponent of the art in Great Britain is universally admitted. The extent of its influence in the development of fine printing is without parallel, and its valuable work is well known to and highly appreciated by all fine printers. As previously stated, it gave extended effect to the style of typography instituted by Mr. Jones; it also rendered much service to the craft by reproducing, or inserting as supplements, many of the best examples of the work of the printers of this and other countries; promoted emulation by its excellent job competitions, besides ably exemplifying the various improvements in process engraving. But what is undoubtedly of still higher importance to the art, this journal inaugurated and gave practical effect to two other eminent developments in fine job composition.

To the influence and enterprise of the *British Printer* was mainly due the successful International Exhibition of Fine Printing held at the Stationers' Hall, London, in October, 1889, one of the results—certainly not the least commendable—of which was the additional impetus given to the question of technical education. The inferior position of English printers in this respect, as compared with their *confrères* on the Continent, where technical schools are maintained by contributions equally apportioned between the employers and the State, was most fittingly pointed out by Mr. Henry Howe Bemrose.

Apart from this, the exhibition afforded the unique opportunity of judging the relative merits and comparing the styles of the work of different countries. Comparison, let it be said, was not altogether unfavourable to the leaders in British fine printing; but, singularly enough, fully two-thirds of the best work in the British section would have been unachievable without the productions of foreign type-founders. Anent this point, the following extract from the address of the Lord Mayor (Sir James Whitehead, Bart.) in opening the exhibition indicates how small had been the assistance home job printers had received from British type-founders during a decade of progress:

> He had for some time been painfully conscious of the fact that this country was not equal to some others in the Art of Printing. But he was inclined to think that this did not arise from any failing so far as the printers themselves were concerned. He feared that there were some behind the printers who were not so desirous of meeting the requirements of the times. He did not want to say a word which could be construed as unkind towards the type-founders of this country; but he was rather inclined to think, from what he had seen, that there was not the disposition to improve their plant, and to provide novelties for their customers, which was to be found in their foreign competitors. He should be within the mark if he said seven-eighths of the material used in the papers issued in connection with the exhibition was of foreign origin. This was a disgrace to England, and if those who were at the back of the printer did not resolve at once that, as far as printing was concerned, Great Britain should at least be put on an equality with other nations, all that he could say was that they were altogether unworthy of their country. He did not believe that the intelligence of the British people would allow them to be behind other countries in the Art of Printing for any lengthened period.

How far Sir James Whitehead's timely words, or the influence of the exhibition, or, yet again, the gradual but sure success of fine printing, may have been instrumental in arousing British type-founders, in some degree, to a sense of their obligations in this respect, it would be difficult to assert; but it is a fact that home type-founders generally and one firm in particular have, during the last few years, endeavoured, and that with considerable success, to remove what could not be regarded other than as a reproach to the commercial enterprise of the first nation of the world.

Under the guiding influence of the *British Printer* this country's job work developed some of its most admirable characteristics. "The deviation from the middle position of the line, chiefly in such a manner that the first part of the line is moved to the left and the second half to the right, whilst they overlap with their ends directed inwards," mentioned as one of the special features of modern English display by Herr Hoffmann, of Berlin, in the *Papier Zeitung* in 1892, was known to and practised by several fine typographers before the *British Printer* had existence; but for the more important principles embodied in the arrangement of display known at the present time as the "Grouping Style" (of which the "deviation from the middle position of the line" was the forerunner), and that placement of borders and rules designated "Geometrical" the two most prominent and admired qualities of British art printing at this date the craftsmen of this country are indebted to the *British Printer*.

Whether the grouping of announcements in fine typography first took definite form in this country or in America is not quite clear. Evidently it was a growth. The practice of arranging wording in comparatively short lines, without any attempt to make the letters at the ends of lines range, but simply filling up the remaining space with ornamental flourishes, has, as is well known, been in vogue amongst artists and architects for many years. And this may probably have some bearing on the question of "grouping" in its typographical aspect. However that may be, allotting two lines to the leading feature of a job when the words were too many to look well in one line, and placing one to the left and the other to the right, resulted eventually in giving two or three lines to the chief item if consisting only of a few words, and placing these to either side preceded or followed by a star or ornament, or wording of minor importance. Judging from the English and American trade journals, this style seems to have been adopted by the craftsmen of both countries at about the same date. There is this difference, however, in the application of the arrangement in the British work it is used with bolder and more striking effect.

In December, 1892, the advantages of grouping display were practically demonstrated in a paper read before the Leicester Technical Class by Mr. Robert Grayson, on "Design and Display in Job Work," and published, with examples, in the first number of the *British Printer* for the year following. Although its principles had been, to an extent, in use amongst home printers for some time anterior to this date, until Mr. Grayson's article appeared the system of grouping cannot be said to have received definiteness.

"The old order changeth, giving place to the new." In comparing "straight line" display with "grouping," one wonders how the "old order" could have obtained so long in job printing; for its principles were as exacting as its appearance was inartistic. Under its sway how often has the sorely-taxed typographer exclaimed, "I can't get anything that makes a good line!" Ten years ago, the "good lines," that is, full ones expanded or condensed according to the subject—and these duly relieved by others of varying length, so selected that no two should clash in length or be alike in character, constituted the first elements of proper display. Their disregard was generally considered an indication of an indifferent collection of types or an indifferent acquaintance with correct typographic effect. The "good lines" are still indispensable to telling effect, but how differently are they formed! The skilful jobbing compositor of to-day, by exercising a little discretion in transposing the phraseology of an announcement—even this is not always necessary—allotting certain portions to different widths in pica ems; giving to the main points two, sometimes three, short lines, instead of one long line, and a few sizes of some two or three series of types, produces a job conspicuous for grace and freedom of style: a job, too, that combines with its artisticality so much vigour that a mere glance conveys to the mind its purport. Truly, the "Grouping Style" is a telling agent in the production of fine printing. The mother-tongue, it is said, gives to the printer larger scope for artistic effect than the language of most other countries: grouping display undoubtedly constitutes the medium by which that effect can be obtained in the fullest degree.

The same master in typography prompted British printers to excel in the use of labour-saving brass rule, combined with appropriate and correct introduction of border and ornament. In the *British Printer* for January-February, 1893, Mr. Grayson commenced the series of "Designs for Job Work," with suggestions for obtaining artistic effects when worked in two or more colours. These have been continued with astonishing fertility and resource in design up to the present year. One of the most remarkable features of this series has been the ingenious and almost limitless manipulation of three-point double medium-face and one-point medium-face brass rule, which used horizontally, vertically, and diagonally, and to form squares, angles, and quadrangles of various sizes, interspersed with ornament and border, has become known as the "Geometrical Arrangement." Says De Vinne, "Ornament is the wine and spice of our typographic feasts: a little is better than a great deal." The "Geometrical Arrangement" is founded on the sound architectural axiom, "Ornament construction, but do not construct ornament."

Since the spread of this system the crude masses of constructed ornament that disfigured much of the British job work a few years ago are now seldom, if ever, seen; and all work that can be considered as worthily representing the efficiency of modern typography is happily free from the error of superabundance of ornamentation. And further, one of the most interesting facts that an examination of the various books of specimens issued by the leading fine printers of this country in recent years reveals is, that not only have they studied the legitimate use of ornament, but that they possess a true perception of what is symmetrical and artistic in design.

The record of these two developments in style brings the subject of Fine Printing in the United Kingdom to its present-day phase.

The flow of telling aids to the production of artistic typography is still strong, and not a month passes that does not witness the introduction of some new agent towards effecting its complete success as a fine art. This increase of material facilitates that diversity of style which is necessary to give suitable effect to the varied nature of the modern typographer's work.

That the next ten years will show as much progress as the past decade seems, at least, improbable. Still, the desire to excel was never more ardent than it is to-day; and that lethargy which so long held sway over the printer and type-founder of this country having given place to action—the "parent of achievement"—who can gauge the future attainments of the art? That the present high state of efficiency will be maintained, if not surpassed, is assured by such splendid exponents of fine typography as the *British Printer*, the *Printing World*, and the art paper edition of the *Printers' Register*.

To every thoughtful craftsman it is apparent that the possibilities of the art are by no means exhausted. As recently as October of last year, Mr. Grayson, in an article on "Curved Borders, and How to Make Them,"[*] disclosed a method which further lessens the restrictions laid upon the artist-printer when dealing with "intractable cold type and brass rule." The increased freedom, however, is only available to those who possess a stereotyping apparatus, and this to some extent may militate against an approach to a general adoption by the craft of the manifest advantages in the direction of a larger scope in design which the method affords.

---

[*] *British Printer*, No. 41.

Fifteen years of well-sustained typographical progress, and what a change has been wrought in the character of British job and book printing! Little short, indeed, of a revolution. The change is complete alike in the appearance of the production and the manner in which it is produced. In composition, "painful plainness," unnatural stiffness, and unappreciativeness of character, have happily given place to tasteful and varied ornamentation, graceful arrangement, and artistic charm in design. The pressman's art is no longer disfigured by a system of "embossing," as detrimental to the type as to the paper, and which necessitated pressing in order to make the work presentable; but proceeding on more scientific principles, he supplements the skill of the designer and compositor with work that brings out delicately, yet firmly, the beauties of modern artistic material.

Compositor and pressman alike can now cultivate the artistic faculty in the highest degree and find ample scope for its expression in the daily routine.

One more point. Beyond the fact of having raised the craftsman's calling to a higher level, the modern development of the "Art Preservative" has an important commercial significance in that it has increased the range of product of the type-founder, the paper-maker, and the ink-maker to an extent well-nigh incalculable.

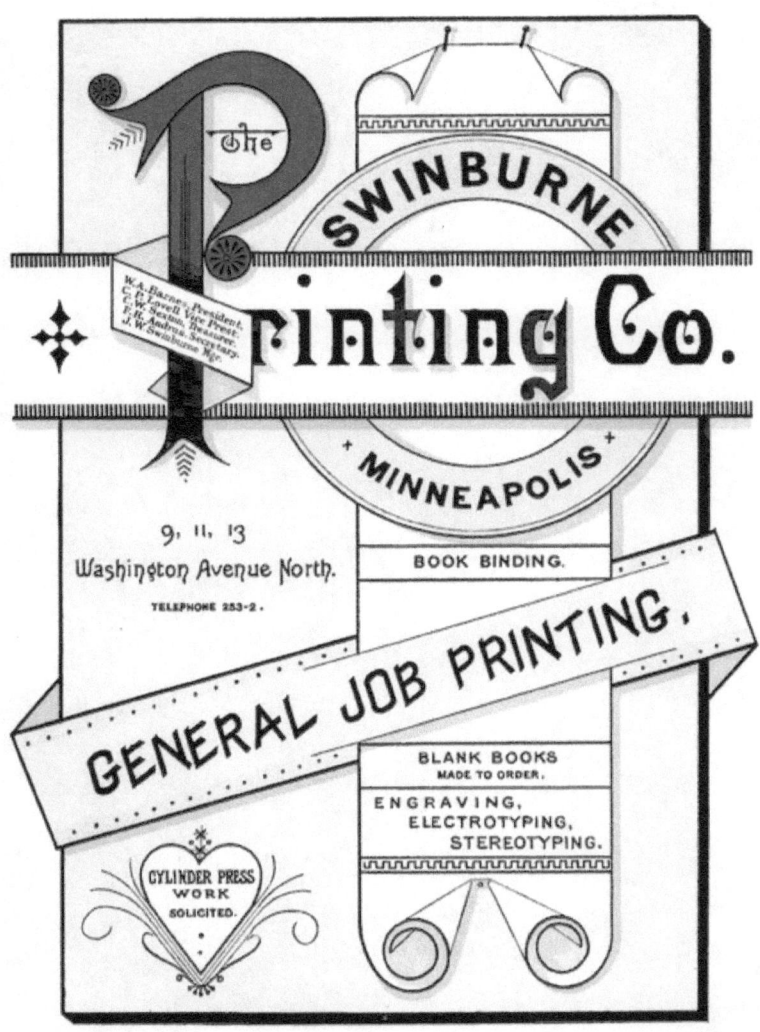

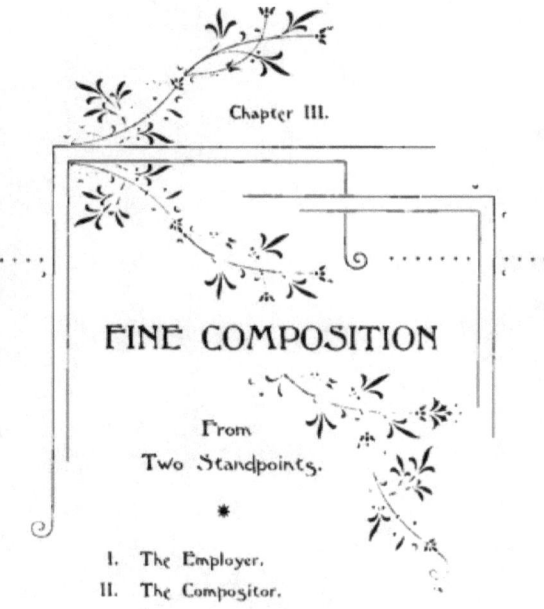

Chapter III.

FINE COMPOSITION

From Two Standpoints.

I. The Employer.
II. The Compositor.

CHAPTER III.

PART I. Good management essential to financial success—Method in arrangement of material and control of its use—The Order Sheet and its value—Designing Fine Work. CLASSIFICATION OF TYPES AND BORDERS: How to arrange fine material so as to ensure facility and proper use. REFERENCE BOOK OF MATERIAL: Its practical utility—Description of compilation. The primary conditions of financial success.

PART II.—The scope of Fine Composition—The necessity for craftsmanship—Practicability of the Development—Intricacy not synonymous with Art. SOME WORKING PRINCIPLES: Artistic Taste—Proportion of Display, with Examples—Uniformity and Contrast of Type Faces—Composing work for Black or Colour, or Rough or Smooth Paper—Spacing—Rising of Quads and Spaces near Blocks—Finish of Details—The advantages of the Compositor of to-day.

EVERY printer of discernment will be prepared to admit the truth of the estimation of a German technical writer who asserts that the men who have attained a high place in the craft, and are happy in the enjoyment of an honourable and wide-spread reputation, understand and understood how to value the worth of theory in connection with practice, from the former of which they gain so many suggestions and useful hints that aid them in the achievement of perfection in the practice of their art. And the workman who does certain things simply because he has seen others do them, or because he has been so instructed, never seeking to know *why* they are so done, or how under varying conditions his tactics would need modification, will not attain and maintain a high place in the typographic art. Undoubtedly, then, theory is indispensable to an intelligent discharge even of the minor operations of either composition or presswork. Yet theory without practice is only a partial success, for in the apt application of theoretical knowledge consists its great value. The promoters of technical education have now recognised the importance of this in providing, in some instances, the typographical teacher and student with plant.

In here treating of some of the principles that underlie the production of fine printing so far as Composition is concerned, it is not intended, therefore, to theorise extensively; but rather to institute a consideration of some of the more important points relating to the subject, as affecting the employer or his immediate representative on the one hand, and the compositor on the other; the basis of such consideration being practical experience.

PART I. THE EMPLOYER.

Taking, then, in proper sequence, the case for the employer, or those who are responsible for good management, either wholly or departmentally. Naturally, the main concern of such is the financial success of their undertaking. "However desirable it may be to take a deep interest in the printer's art to aim at its elevation and advancement, the question of doing a successful business must always be a chief consideration." What is more essential to the achievement of success than system? Nothing. And yet, as is well known to every craftsman of the "rolling stone" order in search of experience (which is sometimes as useful as "moss"), the most striking characteristic of printing offices generally—jobbing offices especially—is the absence of any arrangement worthy the name of system. Custom, but not system.

The old doggerel runs:

The type-founder's friend is the planer hard;

but in these days the type-founder has a greater friend in the employer, manager, or foreman who permits the gross misuse of valuable material so conspicuous in a considerable percentage of modern work. A "free hand" in the use of material may be a very estimable consummation from the compositor's point of view; but, although financial success is as necessary to his welfare as to his chief's, the former oftentimes has regard only to one side of the question—and that not the more important side. To properly use fine material needs fine discretion.

Thus, without enlarging on the results of mismanagement and absence of order, let it at once be said that, to ensure true and lasting success in fine composition, method and control must obtain—method in the arrangement of material; control in its use, as well as in the amount of time expended on the work.

Comparatively few establishments are exclusively devoted to the production of fine typography; generally the latter forms a section of the jobbing department, and to this class the present treatise will more pertinently apply.

Assuming, then, the work to be twofold in character—that is, artistic and commercial—classification is indispensable. Probably this cannot be more effectually obtained than by the adoption of a combined Order and Time Sheet, after the manner of the one given in miniature overleaf.

Suggested size, demy 16mo; the back set the wide way. The utility of this arrangement, apart from its service in the counting-house, is remarkable; and, where the amount of work is considerable, as an agent in keeping things orderly its value is unique. This, however, is by-the-way. The two items, "Style to be Composed" and "Estimated for Setting," and their bearing on fine composition, especially in its financial aspect, call for first consideration.

On account of its expensive nature, not a few master printers regard wrongly, in the main, no doubt the composing department as a sort of necessary evil, and this in cases where the work is of an ordinary description only. How, with work of a more intricate and elaborate character, that undesirable feature would become aggravated it is not difficult to perceive. Hence the necessity for control over the expenditure of time on all jobs, with a view to keeping the cost of composition consistent with the price obtained for the work.

[FORM I.]

ORDER SHEET.

1895.

For whom

Character of Job

Style to be composed   *Ink*

**Estimated for Setting*   hrs.   *Do. Machining*   hrs.

Proof   Revise { *1*
                                  2
                                  3

Complete   *at*   *o'clock.*

Material to be used

No. required   *See that No. and PAPER given out agree with this.*

REMARKS.

* This includes make-up and correcting "House" proof.

For fine work, in the "Style to be Composed" blank can be entered "medium" or "best," according to circumstances. In the former event, the design should be tasteful without tendency to elaborateness; the latter of the terms gives more freedom both in design and with material, and indicates a client who is "not particular to a shilling, so long as the job looks nice." A "best" job may be in one or several colours;

the number of workings would of course govern both design and composition. If a particular design be selected or supplied, it is a simple matter to attach the same to the Order Sheet and fill in "To pattern."

Now a few words as to designing. In some offices this operation is mostly confined to one individual—either the foreman or an expert in typographical design, according to the extent of the department and the

[BACK.]

TIME SHEET.—COMPOSING. ALL TIME ABOVE TWO HOURS TO BE ENTERED.

Date.	Composing.	House Corrections.	Author's Corrections.	Date.	Composing.	House Corrections.	Author's Corrections.

MACHINED on **Machine.**

Date.	Proof.	Working.	Date.	Proof.	Working.

amount of work. The creations of one mind undoubtedly give a distinctive style to the house, a point that De Vinne regards as of high importance; but generally the requirements of clients are as diverse as the nature of the work, and the dissimilar ideas prevailing as to what constitutes "taste" scarcely need be mentioned. Some craftsmen, too, have more aptitude for one class of work than another; and sometimes it is found that the work of one man seldom fails to please a client, whereas that of his fellow will just as seldom secure that particular client's approbation. This, of course, merely involves discretion; and if the foreman be a man of discernment by allotting the work according to the individual *penchant* of the compositor, no difficulty will be experienced in gaining satisfactory results.

Diversity of design certainly has advantages, and is fairly easy of attainment if compositors are permitted to work out their own designs after receiving the foreman's suggestions.

Whether the style cultivated be distinctive or diverse is, after all, not of the highest importance. Oftentimes it is decided by the *clientèle* themselves some are willing to leave their work to the artist-printer's better judgment, while others firmly decline to accept any ideas other than their own. And whether the work be planned out by one or several is also a secondary consideration. But that the work should be planned and that every design before being put in hand for composition should be submitted for approval to a responsible individual, fully cognisant with the price of the job, are in the highest degree essential if the work is to prove remunerative.

This, then, is the safeguard against over-elaboration and waste of time. The system also affords a means of preventing mutilation of material: a point not devoid of significance.

The item "Estimated for Setting" is intended generally to cover the case of competitive work, and the approximate time being entered indicates to the designer and compositor—either or both, as the case may be—the amount of freedom allowed in design and composition in order that the work should yield a fair profit. It may not always be possible to keep strictly within the stated limit. Contingencies may arise, such as a miscalculation in the amount of labour involved, or certain indispensable material not being to hand; but even these fortuitous circumstances can in a measure be modified by selecting borders

Elocution and Dramatic Art.

Private Tuition

By Mr George Upton-Selway.

ROBERT ALLAN,
1 GUTHRIE STREET, EDINBURGH,
OFF CHAMBERS STREET

Leather Merchant

Our Mr
will call upon you in a few days, when the favour
of your orders will be esteemed.

British New Style, 1888.

of large calibre, an avoidance of mitred pieces of rule, and, in the case of two-colour work, a simple make-up for the second forme.

The back of the Order Sheet needs no explanation. The compositor's work being completed, the sheet is returned to the foreman, who subsequently hands it to the pressman as the exigencies of the work demand.

Having systematised the manner of putting work in hand so as to ensure results compatible with the price, in pursuing the consideration of financial success, the next point of importance is the order obtaining in the composing department. Without system here, it need hardly be added, the object of the foregoing arrangements would be entirely frustrated.

The placing of the frames and the various lead and furniture racks, having due regard to light and convenience, is usual, so that on this and matters of minor detail it is unnecessary to dwell. The features of most moment to the careful and proper use of fine material are: first, the orderly method in which the material is arranged; and second, the providing a kind of *vade mecum* of the various types, borders, and vignettes, to which recourse can be had in making designs and for handy reference generally. If the fine material be indiscriminately located, loss of time will naturally result; and from the frequent proofing of initials, borders, or vignettes, "just to see how they will look," precisely the same effect ensues. These two important matters will be treated under the following heads:

> Classification of Borders and Types.
> Reference Book of Material.

CLASSIFICATION OF BORDERS AND TYPES. Mainly the borders and types for fine work come from the foundries of three countries: America, Germany, and Great Britain; and each country's productions should be arranged in frames (dust-proof if available) entirely separate from those utilised for material for ordinary jobbing purposes. This arrangement is convenient alike for composition and distribution. Let it be distinctly understood that the material in these particular frames is for "best" and "medium" work only, and it is unnecessary to so label them. Take the American borders first and put a fairly bold label at the left-hand side of the top case, "American Borders"; then a label of contents in centre of each case, putting one, two, or three combinations according to quantity and number of pieces. Double-double cases answer well for borders, as the small boxes can be used to stand the large pieces on their feet, which prevents contact with each other, and also the possibility of being *thrown* in. American borders and types are cast on the point system, based on the uniform standard of pica adopted by the American Type-founders' Association, twelve points constituting a pica; so that other sizes than six point (nonpareil), twelve point (pica), and their doubles, trebles, or quadruples, require the proper spaces. In the justification of American borders, however, quads or spaces of ten point, fourteen point, and so on, are seldom if ever required. Therefore, immediately following the American borders should be a space case with a good supply of nonpareil, pica, and three-line nonpareil quads; and these not necessarily of American make, Messrs. Stephenson, Blake, and Co.'s standard being, for all practical purposes, identical.

Next to the American can follow the German borders. These are cast on the system formulated by Françoise Ambroise Didot, subsequently to the year 1750 (when Pierre Simon Fournier, foreseeing the great advantages that could be derived from a standard body of type, attempted but failed to create such a desideratum), the standard being cicero, which is rather larger than pica but smaller than english. The system is excellent in principle, all the pieces being cast on cicero and its multiples.* Given a fair supply of the usual spaces, quads, and clumps, even the elaborate German border arrangements are comparatively easy of construction. After the German border cases should follow the case

---

* The American Point System is not a new creation, as is often supposed. It is founded on the lines of Didot's method; but it does not equal the latter in completeness.

containing the requisite spaces and quads. On the left-hand side of the first German border case put a bold label to correspond with that denoting the American section; also a similar distinguishing label at the commencement of the British borders which come next in order. The latter should be followed, if possible, by another nonpareil, pica, and three-line nonpareil space case. How many cases and racks each section of material will require depends of course on the quantity: the arrangement will be found to work satisfactorily whether little or much.

Arrange the founts of type intended for fine work in adjacent racks, keeping series of a letter in consecutive order, beginning with the smallest size. The great advantage a series possesses over a like number of different faces, for modern composition, is too well known to need more than passing mention. Most, if not all, of the founts of German type placed on the British market have been carefully reduced in body to the American standard of points, and so justify to the quads and spaces of that system. Therefore, a distinct arrangement of the types of the different countries is not so essential.

The cases containing the plain and fancy brass rule are best mounted on the frames most convenient for the greater number. Where practicable, it is a good plan to have one case of eight-to-pica thin face rules cut to standard and numbered specially reserved for fine work. For the sake of the material and the pressman care should be taken to avoid, as much as possible, using this particular rule thick way up. The same precaution is necessary with double-thin and light fancy rules. Much of the German brass rule does not join if used wrong way up, owing to a slight bevel at each end of the bottom; its misuse is thus prevented.

REFERENCE BOOK OF MATERIAL.— The material being in order, a means of reference is desirable, for several reasons, the foremost of which has already been stated, namely, to facilitate the designing and arranging of fine work; to this may be added frequent usefulness in taking orders. But some half-dozen copies of such a compilation will be found of much service generally; and the utility of the plan will be still further enhanced by the inclusion of all the general jobbing and book work founts, vignettes, and head and tail pieces. This, on paper, may appear to be what is familiarly known as a "large order"; but even if such a book extend to a hundred and fifty or two hundred pages, a twelve-month's use will more than repay the cost of production. Further, if the composition and presswork of this reference book be promoted when opportunity affords, it can be accomplished with remarkable facility, and serving as a "fill in" is by no means expensive.

Following is a brief description of a book of this character that has proved successful in practical use.

SECTION I.: *Body Founts.* An eight to twelve line paragraph of each size and character—old style and modern—with a line of italic; small sizes, up to pica, in double column, and the remainder, up to double pica, in full measure. These are followed by scripts and fancy founts of sufficient strength for octavo and quarto circulars, similarly arranged; all numbered.

SECTION II.: *Jobbing Founts.* Part I.: Series. Part II.: General. All in double column.

SECTION III.: *Borders and Combination Ornaments.* First, American, English, and German line or continuation borders; in double column, each class numbered and designated. Second, combination borders and filigree ornaments; half page or page as the size and variety of the pieces necessitate to give a practical exhibit.

SECTION IV.: *Initials.* Complete sets, a line each, full measure; of two-colour initials, one each outline and solid.

SECTION V.: *Corners, Block Ornaments, and Vignettes.* This is an extensive section and includes head and tail pieces and coats of arms. Each numbered, and spaced with due regard to distinctness.

SECTION VI.: *Dashes, Brass Rule, and Indices.* A sample of each pattern of brass rule is shown, about twenty ems in length.

The book is demy quarto in size, and the pages are printed on one side of the paper only. At the end of the sections are some twenty perforated blanks for additions. Bound in stiff covers and dark cloth suitable for frequent handling.

The advantage, too, of a few large founts over a considerable number of small ones is as pronounced as that of a series over variety; but the difficulty of always buying extensively is well known to those who guide the affairs of moderate-sized jobbing departments, and who have clients that insist on having certain characters of type used in their work. With small founts it is a very good plan, and saves much valuable time, to have them proofed as received from the foundry on paper of uniform size—say, demy octavo and fastened at the corner, so that their exact extent can be readily ascertained.

In the composition of fine work the primary conditions of financial success are undoubtedly the institution of an orderly arrangement and the obtainment of the best results for a fair amount of labour. Perhaps in no other calling can worse consequences ensue from indifferent management. Fine material placed without distinction; the compositor free to elaborate at will, irrespective of price, or small number or great, and the result will inevitably be far from successful—either financially or in the production of good work. Establish method in arrangement, and that fact in itself is an indication that the material is expected to be used carefully and with discretion.

One of the most successful fine printers of the present day says: "In a properly conducted office, with the right kind of workmen, it may be said that the production of good work costs no more than the inferior. The habit of careful attention once formed, and insisted upon, will in time make 'crooked things straight.'" There are three conditions, however, to the attainment of that typographical Elysium: the properly conducted office, the right kind of workmen, and the insistence on careful attention.

The well-ordered printing office is not merely ideal, as some have proved. The right kind of workmen—none too plentiful, it must be admitted—are not so difficult to obtain under the influence of good order. From lack of system in the office probably quite as many owe their failure to attain competency as from either indifference or negligence. Certainly, if the advantages of a well-conducted composing department do not stimulate the compositor to exhibit some degree of the ability that marks the craftsman it may safely be assumed that he has missed his right avocation. To maintain careful attention, like the other conditions, means work; but the Latin proverb, *Labor omnia vincit*, must possess nothing short of a practical significance to such as desire financial success in Fine Printing.

PART II. THE COMPOSITOR.

The modern development of the "Art Preservative" is to the job compositor a matter of the highest import. While the occupation of his more unfortunate *confrère* "on news" has to some extent been rendered less secure by recent progress, that of the job compositor not only remains unassailed in the ordinary grade, but has so broadened in scope as to afford opportunity for the exercise of artistic genius, combined with increased mechanical skill. The first principles, however, of good type display have in no way suffered depreciation by the opening up of this artistic sphere. To rightly use the increased facilities, in the shape of multitudinous and highly artistic borders, types, and pictorial vignettes, necessitates artistic taste, as well as additional discrimination; a "due appreciation of proportion," too, is indispensable to good designing; but if the "what," "where," or "when" of the type display are not estimated at their proper value, or if correct spacing and finished details are not in evidence, the result is far from successful typographically.

Thus without materially affecting the knowledge that aforetime formed the basis of all good typographical production, the modern development of the art offers to the job compositor opportunity to demonstrate other accomplishments. What are these accomplishments? Primarily, the ability to design and the artistic taste to avoid both incongruity in the selection of type faces and superfluity in ornamentation. Besides these, as already set forth, the facilities this modern development has brought into use involve greater discretion to apply fittingly and increased manipulative skill to handle.

It is well to define the tendency of this increased scope thus concisely, and to emphasise the fact that, in the rudiments, it is not disassociated from ordinary work that attains the standard of good typography; for the compositor not infrequently regards the subject of fine work as a matter needing only the material for its achievement. True, that certain facilities are indispensable; but craftsmanship is pre-eminently indispensable. There is no royal road to the position of the artist-compositor, the harvest corresponds to the tilling; and the young aspirant—or for that matter, any aspirant—cannot afford to disregard the importance of thorough groundwork. The accomplishments may be very interesting, but they must not be allowed to override the necessity of first becoming a good workman. Therefore, let craftsmanship rank first—the ability to design and the cultivation of artistic taste next.

Fortunately for the British job compositor, the development of fine work in this country has advanced generally on sound practical lines. The period of too free use of ornament was happily of short duration, and apart from that drawback and the experiments to produce a variety of chaotic effects, in no essential particular has the progress to a purer and better style been marred. While adopting the best features of American typography, the leading exponents of British fine composition carefully eschewed, in the main, the brass rule twisting craze and other eccentricities that have characterised a considerable proportion of Transatlantic productions. Thus can British printers appreciate to the full the richness of Mr. De Vinne's satire anent the future possibility of the rule-twister's finest efforts finding a place "in our museums by the side of the best decorative work of the Mootka Sound Indian and that of the Fiji Islander."

It is generally conceded, and rightly so, that the British job compositor has not learned much from German type display; but the same cannot be said in respect of the construction of borders. The German examples of border arrangement that influenced British work prior to the introduction of a freer style were always architecturally correct in design and conspicuous for the right use of horizontal and vertical pieces. From the general excellence of finish of German composition the home craftsman has also learned something.

That British job composition has developed to a fine art within the confines of practicability is perhaps its most pleasing characteristic. Not one of the styles marking that development can be designated as impracticable. Ornamental Panel, the Free Style, Grouping, or Geometrical, while decidedly artistic, are all founded on what may be termed legitimate typographical lines, and entirely devoid of extravagance. In no sense can true Art be construed as synonymous with intricacy, eccentricity, or excess of ornamentation. And practicability, above all other considerations, is the most essential feature for the artist-compositor to keep in the forefront. He may occasionally be called upon to produce something bizarre; but experience teaches that this is the exception and not the rule. The work that finds most favour with an enlightened public is not that of an extravagant description; but rather of a class that is striking because of its appropriateness to the subject; is artistic because of the taste exercised in arrangement and the skill that marks its execution.

Under the following heads will be considered some of the chief features of interest to the would-be craftsman in fine composition. In passing, it may be mentioned that in order to design work with that "due appreciation of proportion" and that "perception of truth and beauty in lines" which is the "essence of Art," at least a rudimentary knowledge of drawing will be of much assistance.

BRIDGE OVER THE GRETA.

STEPHENSON'S COTTAGE, NORTH WYLAM.

BY KIND PERMISSION OF
PAYNE JENNINGS, ESQ.

HALF-TONE ENGRAVINGS
FROM PHOTOGRAPHS.

ARTISTIC OR GOOD TASTE.—Perhaps no question is of a more complex nature, or more difficult to define, than that of Taste. "Tastes differ" is a well-established truism. And fortunately so. Without descanting on what is held by the Classical, the Æsthetic, or any other school, to constitute Taste, let it at once be said that for the compositor the best definition is appropriateness. Nothing can make a job more pleasing than the appropriateness of its style and the suitability of its embellishment, if it permit of such; and possibly nothing is sooner deprecated than the compositor's failure to render its appearance harmonious with its purport.

Whether the style desired be plain or ornate, or the result be left to the discretion of the compositor, it can always be appropriate. It is generally his province to select the types, or borders, or vignettes, and on their harmoniousness or incongruity rests the success or failure of the work in respect of taste.

It would be impossible to formulate rules comprehensive enough to cover all the subjects to which the compositor is expected to give fitting effect; but if—with an open mind and determinately resisting the all too prevalent inclination to "go" for the latest new thing in border, type, or ornament, irrespective of its significance—he studiously and assiduously enters into the *spirit* of each particular job he is called upon to produce, he will not be far from a perfectly satisfactory interpretation of artistic taste; an interpretation, too, that will almost invariably find acceptance. By having regard to the nature of the work and the significance of the different characteristics of the material, such anomalies as a quarto circular with six different borders and nine kinds of type in the ten displayed lines; Tudor Blacks in Boniface's annual dinner card; Mikado consorting with Renaissance type faces; a butterfly to fill up the open space in a chrysanthemum design (and the job not in any way connected with the Land of the Chrysanthemum either); and many others "too numerous to mention," will be more rare than they have hitherto been.

FINE PRINTING.

PROPORTION OF DISPLAY.—One of the most telling features of good display is the prominence given to the main points by the proper subjection of the less important matter, thereby ensuring correct perspective. Grouping has done much to break up the sameness of size that at one time marked British display. But even now, with all the advantages of the system named, the practice of bringing forward minor matter to the

---

Dulwich Choral Society.
ESTABLISHED 1891.

Patrons:
SIR JOSEPH BARNBY.
PROFESSOR J. F. BRIDGE, M. Doc.

President:
SIR J. BLUNDELL MAPLE, M.P.

ADMIT TO **Grand**

Evening Concert

COWEN'S
"Rose Maiden"
AND A
SELECTION.

AT

Shawbury Assembly Rooms,
LORDSHIP LANE, EAST DULWICH.

On Wednesday,
9th October,
1895. . . . .

DOORS OPEN AT 7.30. COMMENCE AT 8 P.M.

Reserved Seat, 2/6.

No. 1.— PROPORTION IGNORED.

---

detriment of the leading lines is far more common than it should be; and many compositors fail to realise the importance of the comparative relation of prominent and subordinate display.

The two examples here given furnish practical illustration of what is meant by proportion. Although the main lines in example No. 1 are as large as those in No. 2, the former bears no comparison with the latter either for emphasis or readableness. As will be seen, subjection of the less important matter does not imply such minuteness as would render the wording difficult to read; but simply by using small yet clear-faced types—in preference to types so large as to clash with the main lines—emphasis is given to the chief points without causing the subordinate matter to suffer detraction. Indeed, by the additional space and a more compact appearance the subordinate matter is likewise enhanced.

No. 2. PROPORTION OBSERVED.

One class of work only is here illustrated, but the compositor, once having grasped the principle, will find its general application comparatively easy. With jobs of importance, a few minutes spent in sketching out the prominent display and locating the minor parts will be time well laid out.

For general guidance in selecting condensed, square, or extended types, the following is an excellent rule: "Endeavour to use a type which in shape is somewhat similar to the shape of the card or paper it is going to be printed on. Supposing it to be a large card, long way on, then you would be right in using a square or slightly extended series. If the announcement is short way on, then a slightly condensed series could be used. This produces a much better appearance than if they were reversed."*

UNIFORMITY AND CONTRAST OF TYPE FACES.—The correct model in illustration of proportion also contains two other principles worth noting, namely, the uniformity of style of the main lines and the contrast produced by the different character of the remainder. These are two of the most pleasing, as well as most important, traits in modern display. To say that uniformity is enhanced by contrast in an individual job seems somewhat paradoxical, although in reality it is not so. The most successful fine composition is that limited to some three or four faces of type: uniformity characterises the main lines, which may be either moderately light or moderately dark, capitals or lower case; contrast is obtained by relieving the main lines, if light, with small type of a rather heavy description; if dark, then with small type of a clear and well-defined stamp. Lower case small type to main lines of capitals, or *vice versa*, is a very good rule. In either event the result is harmonious, and the contrast gives vigour to the uniform display, while the artistic effect of light and shade is assured.

Chasteness, elegance, novelty, and force are all obtainable from the varying degrees of uniformity and contrast in composition; hence these are important features and deserve the compositor's closest attention.

As much as possible avoid extremes. The proximity of very light and very heavy types; jobs set all in capitals, or all in lower case; lines of quaint capitals (unless the work demands such); letters with tails next to letters with the down stroke; or anything tending to incongruity

* Robert Grayson. *British Printer*, Jan.-Feb., 1893.

or indistinctness should be carefully eschewed. Any ornament that interferes with the perfect readableness of the text is an ornament misused.

COMPOSING WORK FOR BLACK OR COLOUR, OR ROUGH OR SMOOTH PAPER. These are matters that need consideration before commencing to design or compose work. If it is proposed to print a job in black ink only, the composition would be affected to the extent of guarding against the use of too heavy type, border, or ornament. Jobs for colour permit of a bolder treatment; and, unless the colour has been decided upon prior to composition, one of a deeper or lighter hue, according to the strength of the composition, can be used. Again, the composition for jobs in bronze blue, dark brown, or dark green should not be so heavy as for either light or medium browns or pale blue.

With designed work for more than one colour it is often possible to decide on borders, vignettes, or initials for the second or third working, and in this event a saving of time is effected by omitting such from the key forme in the first instance.

While art paper admits of the finest and most delicate class of types and borders being used to advantage, their beauty would be entirely lost on antique papers, or on those of the imitation canvas, ribbed, flowered, or embossed description. For papers of this kind the composition should be free from light-faced material and over-elaboration. On rough or uneven-surfaced papers, by a simple grouping style of arrangement of such types as "Erratic," "Childs," "De Vinne," "Lafayette," or "Mikado," and suitable silhouette ornaments, some excellent and effective typography can be achieved.

SPACING. Although this subject has been so much written about, the percentage of compositors who space correctly is far from satisfactory. Take, for example, a list of names and addresses and one will probably more often find it spaced even thicks:

      IRREGULAR BADSPACE, Esq., M.P., 48, Uneven Square, W.,

than with two thicks between the capitals, an en quad after one point (unless it precedes a letter that shows a slight margin, like the "W" above, then a thick space), and a thick space after two points:

REGULAR GOODSPACE, Esq., M.P., 56, Restful Avenue, W.

The latter entails picking up one space more than the former, certainly; but the difference to the technical mind is worth much more than the single movement it takes to its accomplishment; and, further, it is the mark of distinction between the compositor who uses his brains and the one who does not.

Good spacing is essential in fine composition. For display lines whether condensed, square, or extended, capitals or lower case the correct space between words is equivalent to the thickness of the average letter of the fount, say an "e." To be quite clear on this point: in spacing a line of capitals, the space should be equal to the capital "E"; if a lower-case line, then equal to the lower-case "e." This average space should not be exceeded; rather would a little less be better than more. Of course with letters that show a slight margin, such as A, F, L, and so on, the space can be somewhat modified; also before and after quotation marks, commas, and fullpoints, except where the latter complete sentences. To treat these points entirely as space is as objectionable as to ignore the addition they make to the space; generally, if they be calculated at a half, the "happy medium" will be attained. This is also a very good rule to observe with catch lines, modifying a little according to the length.

No standard can be set up to govern the leading or whiting out of job work, owing to its diverse nature. To regulate the position of the different lines so that they appear well balanced and distinct is an art which can only be gained by practice and careful observation. Good spacing may be fittingly described as one of the pleasures of typography, and one that every compositor who takes the craftsman's pride in his work will hasten to avail himself of. Bear in mind that haphazard spacing has not even the quality of time-saving in its favour, so that it results either from ignorance or carelessness.

RISING OF QUADS AND SPACES NEAR BLOCKS. Doubtless there are very few craftsmen who have not been at times greatly exercised by the rising of spaces in formes containing blocks. Every care has been taken in justification; the blocks have been tested and gauged, yet all to very little purpose: a hundred runs or so and the old disfigurement. Here is a suggestion that appeared in the *American Pressman* a short time ago, and one that practice has proved generally most effectual. Cut pieces of three-sheet card about a pica or three nonpareils in width; affix with paste near the *bottom of the four sides* of the block, if type all round, or to those sides which have type next to them. This is rational enough when it is considered that the lock-up has a tendency to contract the mount of a block; and this contraction must of necessity be more pronounced at the bottom than at the top where the plate is.

FINISH OF DETAILS. — "Trifles make perfection, but perfection is no trifle." Perhaps it is just bordering on Idealism to talk of perfection in connection with the "Art Preservative." Certainly, faultless typography is not altogether unknown; but it is very rarely met with. Therefore it will be better to take the word "perfection" in the sense of "completely skilled." It is easy to perceive that work may be both skilful and finished, yet on a critical examination disclose slight defects in letter or border which would render the term "perfection" in the sense of faultlessness inapplicable. "Look after the little things: the big things will look after themselves." The details are the "little things" or the "trifles," as you will that finished make, or unfinished mar, the full success of the compositor's work. A job may be well designed, the display may be effective and in good proportion; but if it also be characterised by bad spacing, imperfectly joined rules, slipped letters, or faulty lock-up, then those "little things" that would have made it "completely skilled" have been neglected.

Than the treatment of details, nothing sooner distinguishes the craftsman from the bungler. The craftsman quickly discerns the faulty quad or space or other matter that would mar the finish of his work, and just as quickly removes the fault or discards the defective piece; brings into operation the thought and care necessary to good justification and make-up; notes the condition of the stone before sliding his job, because he knows that grit and dirt will not only give the pressman trouble but spoil the material; and then the sidestick and quoins duly in place, with a final look to see that everything is where he intended it should be, without any fancy action or planer rataplan, he drives the wedge or applies the key just sufficiently to ensure that all in the forme shall be quite secure and yet as solid when finally planed as it was before lock-up.

Does his work take longer than that of the compositor, so-called, who with fussy haste takes anything that comes first to hand, whether good, bad, or indifferent; expects the mallet and shooter or key to make passable his faulty work by a lock-up twice as tight as it ought to require, only to be bashed down by, or into the face of, the planer; and then capers round the stone to "sight" his job, with an air worthy a marksman, when, forsooth, he has taken no pains to ensure its straightness? Experience gives an emphatic "No!"

Follow the two formes to the machine-room. An impression is taken of the craftsman's work: every join is properly made, no letters or points perforate the paper; a few touches perhaps on account of a little unevenness in wear, is all the pressman finds necessary to ensure a most satisfactory result so far as the type portion is concerned. But try the bungler's work. If the pressman is an expert he will quickly perceive that something is wrong with the composition or lock-up, and either he or the "genius" who slung it together will have two or three journeys in order to get the thing put right. Or, maybe, the pressman will proceed with the make-ready only to find, after an hour's labour, probably more, that the last state of that job is worse than the first.

A SPECIMEN OF Chromo-Typography.

"Azaleas."

EIGHT WORKINGS.

It is needless, however, to enlarge unduly on the dire results of badly finished work. It would scarcely be necessary to touch on the point were it not that, judging from the difficulty one encounters in leading the "young idea" into right grooves, the bungler's style is all too attractive. Hence it cannot be too strongly urged that just as "good wine needs no bush," so the craftsman's work needs nothing fantastical to supplement its intrinsic value.

Another cause of inferiority in the finish of work is the too frequent habit of leaving, after making corrections, portions of lines, words, letters, or points sticking up. Instead of putting all such carefully into place with the cushions of the fingers—not with the nails—it is oftentimes left to the planer after the quoins have been tightened with the fingers. The result is seen in i's without dots, f's without curves, thick letters, and points piercing the card or paper.

Formes containing blocks as well as type should be planed in this way: First gently tap down the type, keeping quite clear of the blocks—and initials, if mounted on wood—then tap the latter down with a smooth quoin. The reason for this is, that when blocks are "levelled up" for machine, partly owing to the nature of the mounts and partly owing to the larger surface presented for impression, they stand rather above the type; thus, to plane down both at one operation would cause the type to rise to the level of the blocks. Especially is this separate planing important with half-tone process blocks, for these present a much fuller surface for impression than line engravings or woodcuts.

Complete mastery over the working principles here indicated will be by no means an insurmountable task to the compositor of average tact and intelligence. No matter how exhaustive the instruction or extensive the illustration of a subject, it would not avail the man who does not trouble to think for himself. It has been well said that the "secret of successful and thorough knowledge of the Art of Printing lies as much in what you teach yourself as in what others teach you." To such as will, the acquisition of that knowledge presents no difficulty to-day. Even if the lines have not fallen to some in the "pleasant places" where fine composition is achieved, technical education and trade journals of unprecedented excellence offer advantages for the fullest acquaintance with all that is best in the craft. Every subject of importance to the compositor's art receives investigation and elucidation; while his faculties are further stimulated by object lessons of surpassing merit and opportunities to put his ideas into practical shape.

"Mysteries of the Art"! The term is now a satire. The only mystery that remains is, that with all the advantages of the period no authority admits there is an abundance of careful and efficient craftsmen! Efficiency, however, is "not attained by sudden flight." The good influences of the last few years' progress have not been in vain, and to-day the evidences of "toiling upward" are decidedly in the compositor's favour. Be assured that sterling worth will not long remain unknown or unappreciated, for the time has not yet come when it can be said there is no room at the top.

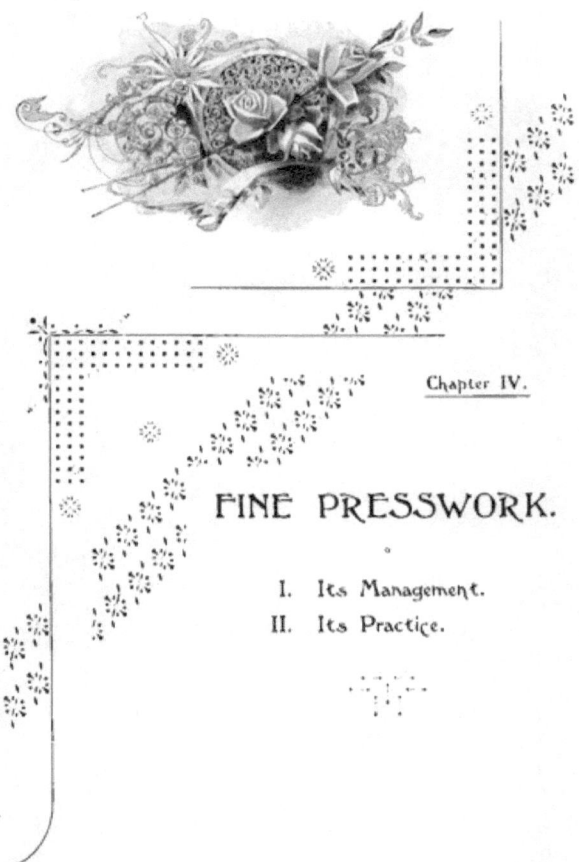

Chapter IV.

FINE PRESSWORK.

I. Its Management.
II. Its Practice.

CHAPTER IV.

PART I. A remarkable Make-Ready and its results—The utility of Hard Packing, Overlays for Cuts, and smooth Dry Paper—The term "Presswork." MANAGEMENT: The province of the Order Sheet—Arrangement and Expedition—Drying Cabinets—Machinery for Fine Presswork—The importance of Good Pressmen—The Supply of Rollers—Papers for Fine Work—The Commercial Aspect of Fine Presswork.

PART II. Principles of Impression and Rolling in Platen and Cylinder Machines.
FINE WORK AT PLATEN MACHINE:
  The fitness of the forme for machining—The operations involved in Making Ready a quarto circular in two colours and two tints—Mixing and Working of Tints—Etc.
FINE WORK AT CYLINDER MACHINE:
  Bearings and Bearers—Packing the Bearers, and Why—The operations involved in Making Ready eight pages of Fine Work—Two Dressings of Cylinder—Etc.
Making Ready Process Blocks—Making Ready Engravings: One, two, and three sheet Overlays—Method of Cutting a three-sheet Overlay (Illustrated)—Care and Treatment of Rollers—Embossing: Three methods—Etc.

HILE modern typographical progress has wrought so great change in the character of job and book composition, its influence on presswork has been correspondingly great. The old-time pressman knew nothing of hard packing, of overlays for cuts, or of calendered and coated papers. With woollen blanket and paper thoroughly wet, the "sweeping lever his commands obey'd" so well that, however "light o'er the form the sheeted tympans" flew, it never failed to administer an impression decidedly heavy.

And undoubtedly that was the treatment best suited to the quality of the type and the coarseness of the illustration of that age. But in due course, as material improved and engraving became finer and more artistic in finish, the woollen blanket and the wetting process had to give place to methods better calculated to enhance the beauty of the type-founder's, the engraver's, and the paper-maker's productions.

How great and far-reaching has been the influence of Joseph A. Adams's remarkable fortnight's work in making ready the first forme of "Harpers' Illustrated Bible" it would be almost impossible to compute. That fortnight is certainly a period of great interest to the art of fine presswork. Eminent engraver and artist, he well understood all the points essential to a perfectly successful picture; and "day after day he cut, scraped, rubbed, and strained a new sheet over the whole," eventually not only producing the finest work that America or any other country had seen up to that time, but, what is of more general importance, evolving the principle of hard packing and developing the system which obtains to-day of preparing overlays for cuts. That the Messrs. Harper were alarmed at the time the work took it is easy to believe; however, apart from the resulting technical advancement, it is interesting to note that this magnificent production "enriched the projector and made the publishers comfortable."

Another notable outcome of Mr. Adams's work was an improvement in the direction of a greater amount of rolling capacity and more perfect distribution of ink. The first numbers of "Harpers' Illustrated Bible" were printed on two-roller machines and were treble rolled to each impression. Owing to the success of the work a six-roller machine was built, thus rendering it possible for a sheet to be printed at each revolution.

Some few years later—about 1850—when the Gordon treadle machine for job work was invented, it was found, as already adverted to in a preceding chapter, that by using smooth polished paper, not only was it possible to print without wetting the paper, but that cuts could be printed with a clearness and sharpness not obtainable with wet paper. Then, as machinery improved in strength and rigidity and rolling capacity; as the successful development of process engraving popularised illustration; and as job work assumed a form at first striking on account of its ornateness and brilliancy of colouring, but later for its gracefulness and quiet harmony; the great utility of hard packing, overlays, and printing on smooth dry paper is revealed in the fact that these are the generally accepted media for giving the best and finest effects to the pressman's art.

However, although new methods obtain in presswork, and cylinder and platen machines have almost entirely supplanted the hand-press which gave currency to the term, it is worthy of note, in passing, that "presswork" still designates the operation of making ready and taking impressions from formes of type or blocks. But beyond the retention of the term there is very little in common between the productions or the qualifications of the old-time pressman and those of his present day successor, especially where the work of the latter comes within the definition of fine presswork.

The present high state of efficiency of machinery and production could only have been attained by a liberal circulation in technical literature of the various improved methods resulting either from investigation, experience, or that "mother of invention," necessity. Fortunately, there has been no stint in the dissemination of technical light. And to-day every topic of interest, from machine construction and colour harmony to the cleaning of rollers and manner of handling sheets to ensure accuracy of lay, receives its share of attention, either at the hands of the technical instructor or the technical writer, until one not unnaturally asks, What is there new in Presswork?

The purpose, however, of this dissertation on fine presswork is not to propound new theories, even were that possible, but to treat of some important practical matters anent the subject matters which, though probably for the most part dealt with before, in this case having to their recommendation some degree of technical and financial merit, may be of value to the chief or head of the department as well as to the pressman.

On this account the subject will be taken in two considerations, coincidently with the foregoing chapter on " Fine Composition."

I. THE MANAGEMENT OF FINE PRESSWORK.

The method of putting work in hand, the convenience of arrangement that ensures reasonable expedition, and the suitability of the machinery, together with an efficient supply of good rollers, are among the items of first importance to those whose desire is the production of high-class work. Given these, and the right kind of workmen—an essential though mentioned last by no means the least important, of course the master printer or his representative may not unreasonably expect good typographical results from an expenditure of time that does not prohibit fair remuneration.

As to method of putting work in hand, take first the points affecting presswork as indicated in

THE ORDER SHEET. On reference to this it will be found there are several items for the guidance of the pressman. First he ascertains what the job is; whether it is in colour or black, as well as the quality of ink, and whether a good or rough proof or a job for running, and in the latter case the number of runs.

With the Order Sheet the pressman should of course have any additional instructions the particular work renders necessary. For instance, if a job contains blocks, whether such are to have one, two, or three sheet overlays cut, or are only to be levelled up. In this way the exigencies of price and the time for completion can be met.

After submitting a made-ready example for approval, the running off can be proceeded with. On completion the pressman fills in the particulars required, attaches a copy of the work to the Order Sheet, and deposits the same in the place assigned for that purpose.

It hardly need be added that the Order Sheet is of considerable service to the pressman. Concisely before him he has the principal information respecting his work, and that information once read by and for himself is probably more effectual in avoiding the possibility of forgetfulness than verbal instructions twice or even thrice given.

ARRANGEMENT WITH A VIEW TO EXPEDITION.—This, in the main, is obviously a question of environment; but two suggestions may not be out of place in this connection. The first is as to the manner of supplying the pressman with the requisite paper or card for the work in hand, while the second has reference to the disposal of that work during or after the process of printing. If the pressman, having received instructions for the work required of him, has to go to the manager, or foreman, or whoever has charge of the stock, for the material for that work, and, having obtained the same, wait until the cutting or trimming is accomplished, the "arrangement" is scarcely conducive to expedition. Yet, strange to say, that custom is not altogether unknown in some printing offices. But digression aside. If an Order Book be kept in the counting-house or warehouse in which are entered the particulars of name, material, and number, corresponding with those on the Order Sheet, it is a simple matter for the warehouseman to work from this book in giving out paper or card. Then, after writing quantity and name on the top sheet, it should be put on or in a paper rack, contiguous to the press-room, where it is convenient and ready for the pressman to take.

Just as unfinished details mar the beauty of composition, so off-set mars the beauty of presswork. Especially is fine presswork liable to off-set, on account of the high finish of the material, unless due care is taken to prevent contact with the newly-printed matter. This is usually accomplished either by insetting or laying out. Against the effectualness of the former nothing can be said; but for the lighter class of fine work the insetting can be dispensed with, while the cleanliness and orderly disposal of the printed work are ensured, by providing

DRYING RACKS for its reception. Perhaps "Drying Cabinet" would be a more fitting term to apply to a practical contrivance that has been found to answer well in use and of which the following is a brief description. With the exception of eight upright strips (two at the back and three on each side, to prevent the printed sheets from slipping out), the framework of the cabinet is open to admit air freely, and is nineteen inches wide, two feet long, and three feet two inches high. This is the size used with machines up to demy folio, and it takes in seven lattice-work trays three inches apart, so that five hundred sheets, say of demy folio art paper, can be placed upon each tray without causing friction in pushing in or drawing out. The trays and grooved slides for same are made of American white wood, which is strong and does not warp easily. The cabinet is solid at the top and therefore useful to the pressman in many ways; but is used primarily to put the trays on when work is in progress. Commencing with the first tray, the pressman lays the sheets out over the tray as taken from the machine; so that, assuming the job were an octavo circular, four sheets would be put down before others were laid upon them. After laying the sheets to such depth as would ensure freedom from off-set, the next tray is taken, and so on. Four small wheels at the bottom of the legs are fixed to run direct only, which enables the pressman to easily run the cabinet back when necessary to get round the machine, while any liability to push the cabinet on to the fly wheel from the side is obviated.

It is a very good plan to have one of these drying cabinets to each machine; above demy they are best if built to take the trays the oblong way. Their utility is self-evident. As to the cost, it is by no means great. Most printers' furnishers would be prepared to supply (stained and varnished outside) the folio and crown sizes, say for an order of ten, at about two pounds each.

MACHINERY FOR FINE PRESSWORK.—Pre-eminently in machinery for fine printing "the best is the cheapest." Hard packing, half-tone engravings, and coated papers are well calculated to bring out the capabilities of the machine, whether platen or cylinder. How in the highest degree rigidity of impression and perfect ink distribution are essential, those who are at all familiar with fine work can fully appreciate. If to those points can be added accurate and well-balanced motion and simplicity of construction—having due regard to efficiency—then you have a machine suitable for the production of fine presswork.

For light artistic job work up to a quarto circular, platen machines with the disc principle of distribution and what is called the "clam-shell" or "pair of shears" motion of type-bed and platen are in every way eminently suitable; but heavy type formes, half-tone engravings, or blocks of solid or almost solid surface can only—with at least one notable exception, in which the disc principle is supplemented by a duplex distributor in addition to an attachment for regulating the rotation of the disc, and the platen is mounted on an ingenious arrangement of wedge-shaped bearings, which facilitate increasing or decreasing the impression besides providing the requisite strength for any class of platen presswork—be satisfactorily printed on machines having cylindrical distribution and in which the platen has a direct slide up to the forme. The liability of the first-mentioned class of machine to a heavier impact at bottom than top of the type-bed and platen, as well as the system of distribution, renders it unsuitable for work requiring great firmness of impression and considerable body of colour; nor was it intended for such work.

The extraordinary distributing power of a demy-folio platen machine with cylindrical distribution is shown in the fact that the cylinder, thirty inches in circumference, revolves three times to each impression; so that the surface of distribution is ninety inches—more than twice that of an ordinary double-demy cylinder machine with a twenty-five inch slab, as the inkers do not cover the whole of that surface. Another advantage—an important one, by the way—that the system of cylindrical distribution possesses is the regulation of the quantity of ink for uneven formes. For instance, it not infrequently happens that one side of the forme requires perhaps double the amount of ink to the other side, or one of two quarto pages is much heavier than the other; by regulating the ductor accordingly, these inequalities can in great measure be coped with successfully.

To ensure rigidity, a cylinder machine for fine work should have extra wide bowl rails, say four of three-and-a-half inches for a quad-crown, besides a frame of suitable strength, and the frame should certainly be solid or afford substantial support immediately beneath the cylinder. The foundation for the machine should be a thick wooden frame and crosspiece well set in concrete—on this the machine will be found to run with an easy and regular motion and practically free from vibration, which means a saving in wear and tear. With a reciprocating distribution cylinder or receptor drum (which receives the supply of ink from the ductor vibrator and is thence transferred to the slab by the receptor vibrator), five inkers, and two geared and two ungeared riders; together with the modern arrangement of seven distributor holders on each side, which can also be utilised for varying the position of the distributors or wavers to suit a forme requiring more ink on one side than the other, the distributing and rolling capacity is fairly satisfactory. Four of the holders mentioned are raised by lifters as the carriage of the machine runs out, and thus contact between the distributors and the forme is prevented. Then if the machine has a slab with rounded end, a double-inking motion, and balanced flyers, it may be said to possess most of the features desirable in a machine for high-class work.

With a machine of this description that has power and distribution sufficient to print a book forme of sixteen pages, say of foolscap quarto, each containing a half-tone block or woodcut, under a hard-packed cylinder, no fear need be entertained as to its suitability for any other class of work that may be required of it. Such a machine—or press, as our American *confrères* prefer to term it—may cost a hundred pounds more than one of indifferent quality and capacity; but the delays and the poorness of the work resulting from so-called cheap machinery would soon convince the master printer that there is such an element as false economy.

Just a word as to the pressman. Having expended a large amount in order to ensure a good machine, see that it is in charge of a good man. In fact, a "man who is *more* than the machine." To once again re-echo De Vinne's words: "The damage that the machine receives from men who do not know how to handle it is great. Upon the pressman, more than any other workman, depends the credit of your office."

THE SUPPLY OF ROLLERS.—Next to good pressmen and good machinery, what is more indispensable in the production of fine press-work than good rollers? In this age it is not difficult to obtain fairly good rollers, though the perfect roller, like the perfect man, is a *rara avis*. It is a very good plan, and not the most expensive, to contract with a firm of repute for the periodical renewal of rollers. But whether obtained in this way or another, it is important in fine work that the supply be ample and of the best quality. A spare set of rollers to each machine will afford a selection of the most suitable for the different kinds of work, and generally save much time and trouble.

PAPERS FOR FINE WORK.—Selecting suitable paper for the various classes of work is hardly the simple matter some are inclined to think. With the medium grade of art paper, as a rule, little difficulty is experienced either in the printing or drying. It is moderately porous, and therefore the ink dries into the surface. But the hard, highly-burnished —"exhibition polish," in fact—class of paper is often disastrous to the technical success of the work. Apart from its slippery nature, it is bad for ink, the best quality of which looks little better than a pale stain; and in book work with cuts it is almost an impossibility to get type or picture on to its hard, shiny, over-calendered surface without a stippled appearance that is anything but artistic. The most suitable coated and calendered papers are moderately absorbent without being too limp, and have a well-finished and even surface, neither dull nor too glossy.

As a master printer recently pointed out, "Nor must the *quality* of the paper only be considered — its *condition* may be, and frequently is, a source of much annoyance. Instances have occurred where samples have been obtained for the purpose of proofing, and having come out satisfactorily the bulk has been ordered, and yet when the job came to be worked a difficulty has at once confronted the pressman. Something was wrong. The appearance was entirely different from the proof, while apparently the paper was the same. On close examination, however, it was found that the sample was drawn from old stock, while that supplied for the job was new. Such is a common cause of trouble, and one which often tests to the utmost the ingenuity of the most accomplished pressman. In obtaining samples for proofing it is advisable, therefore, to procure, if at all possible, sheets of the identical paper that will be used. This, of course, cannot be done in large orders where the paper has to be made. The tendency is, when a difficulty of this kind arises, to put the fault upon the ink-maker, who, like all others, at times deserves censure, but is frequently unjustly blamed." [*]

The commercial aspect of fine presswork is of some interest. The large amount of time that might be expended on such work, the costly nature of the material, together with the risk of spoilage, render imperative a strict surveillance over its cost. Having assured oneself of the competence of the pressman, the only satisfactory foundation on which to form a computation is the actual time spent on the work. The prevalence of estimating oftentimes necessitates a fixed price before the work is put in hand for execution, and in this case the pressman, no

Printers' Register, August, 1894.

more than the compositor, should be allowed to exert his talent in the wrong direction. If the client must have his work at a certain price, and the pressman spends hours in cutting overlays for blocks when that price would only allow for levelling up, it is hardly necessary to say who it is that "pays the piper." Happily, the intelligence of the age tends to an unprecedented appreciation of high-class and meritorious work. Still, it is not derogatory to the pressman's honour as a skilled workman if he be expected to do his part towards keeping the cost of work, in certain cases, to such limits as would allow a fair profit in the prospective remuneration; and this, too, without undermining in the slightest degree the best of working principles, namely, that "What is worth doing, is worth doing *well.*"

It is possible to spend industriously six or seven hours over the make-ready of a script circular, if the client cannot accept anything short of a perfect production; but the pressman would not be justified in expending that amount of time, nor would the master printer be justified in charging the client with it, unless the latter or others affected by its quality could appreciate the work at its right value and were willing to pay accordingly. The same illustration holds good all the way through the various grades of fine presswork. Starting with the fundamental basis that all the work is to be creditably done, the stages of "medium" and "best" should be attained as the remuneration ascends in corresponding ratio. If combined with that arrangement are cleanliness and good order in the machine-room, and the other essentials already indicated, the artistic and financial aspects of fine presswork need not be irreconcilable.

II. FINE PRESSWORK: ITS PRACTICE.

Although in the proper working of a hand-press there is much that forms a useful rudimentary knowledge even to the system of modern presswork, the manipulation of the hand-press now so seldom finds a place—certainly not an important place—in the pressman's routine that no further explanation is needed to account for its absence from this treatise on the practice of fine presswork. For the most part, if not entirely, modern job, pamphlet, and book printing is accomplished on two classes of machines—platen and cylinder. As is well known, these present different principles of impression and rolling. In the former, although in some makes the type-bed is stationary and in others it swings on a shaft to meet the forward motion of the platen, the principle of impression is the same: the whole surface of the forme is printed at once. In the latter, the impression is gradual, each part of the forme being printed as contact is made in the rotary action of the cylinder. And while in the platen machine the inking of the forme is accomplished by the rollers passing over it, in the cylinder machine the forme passes to and fro under the inkers.

With the manner of producing work on these two types of machines it is proposed to deal. To be comprehensive, it will be advisable to take an average example of fine work for each class of machine, and go through the various operations involved in the production of such example; then to follow with the method of printing cuts, half-tones, the treatment of rollers, and other matters relating to presswork generally, which in some instances may be applicable to either platen or cylinder machine or both.

FINE WORK AT PLATEN MACHINE.—The German supplement in this work furnishes a very good example for this section, for more than one reason. Being in four workings, an opportunity is afforded to touch on the method adopted to ensure register; and having tints as well as colours, the manner of obtaining and working the tints will add to the utility of the treatise. The colours are bronze blue and chocolate, and the tints buff and blue. The key forme is that for bronze blue, and the first consideration is as to its fitness for the machine. The pressman who understands what a forme should be like when ready for the

Spicer Brothers, Limited,

HAVE ONE OF THE LARGEST AND MOST COMPREHENSIVE STOCKS IN EVERY DEPARTMENT OF THE TRADE

Printing Papers in Reels and Reams.

White and Coloured, in every quality.

PROPRIETORS OF THE FAMOUS "ORIQUE" BOARDS

Writing Papers.

Machine and Hand-made, for all purposes.

Exquisite Art Papers.

White, Tinted and Duplex.

AGENTS FOR 288 AND 424 MILL TINTED PAPERS

Brown and Wrapping Papers.

SPICER BROTHERS, Limited,

Paper Makers.

19, New Bridge St., London, E.C.

ALSO AT
MANCHESTER,
GLASGOW AND
NEWCASTLE

GROUPING DISPLAY.

machine has made himself master of a highly important detail. After wiping the back of the forme with the open hand, it is put on the imposing surface for planing down. A gentle tap at the corners with the shooting-stick and a smooth quoin discloses whether it is solid or at all sprung. If sprung, the compositor's attention would of course be required; but if solid it can be planed in the ordinary way, using the handle of the mallet, which supplies quite enough power to ensure a properly justified and locked-up forme being down on its feet. On no account should a forme be taken to machine that does not present a firm face to moderate planing. From a springy forme it is impossible to produce good work. By-the-way, too, when the formes of any job of two or more workings in which good register is a desideratum, are not imposed in machine chases, it is advisable to lock up from the bottom as well as the side, and thus anticipate the possibility of shifting in the event of the forme being unlocked after the make-ready has been commenced or part of the job completed.

Rollers for bronze blue should not be hard or dry, but fairly tacky. Having ascertained that the rollers, ink ductor, and type-bed are perfectly clean, the dressing of the platen is proceeded with. According to the height the platen is set would be the number of sheets and thickness of the cardboard. In the present case two sheets of 25-lb. double crown are taken and inserted under the bottom tympan clip; under these sheets, next to the platen, is put four-sheet cardboard of good quality; and then, drawing the sheets tightly over the cardboard, they are placed under the top clip. With the palette knife, a small quantity of ink is put on the rollers and run up. Now the forme is put on and secured, the gripper fingers set well clear of the forme, the impression lever set back, and a rather light pull on 25-lb. double crown taken. From this pull most of the inequalities of type and border are apparent, and recourse must be had to underlays for the low parts so as to ensure equal rolling and even impression. The forme is placed face down on the machine board (on which some odd sheets of paper have been put to protect the face), and the weak parts are underlaid with paper of such thickness as will secure the desired equality of surface. Underlays should be a little smaller than the letter or piece of border it is intended to bring up, and the merest touch of paste will suffice to keep them fast. Underlaying cannot be too carefully done, and owing to its effectualness should be thoroughly accomplished, even to the use of tissue paper if necessary. "It is possible to get moderate results when overlaying is omitted, but impossible where low places in the forme are not equalised with its body. In brief words, skilful underlaying is the key to good presswork."[a]

Another impression is now taken, and such further defects as would be best treated from underneath having been attended to, all is ready for the first pull on the tympan sheet. The appearance of the four em cicero border is generally satisfactory; hence a cut-out overlay is not necessary for this forme. Here and there letters, or rule corners, or a piece of border will be improved by a thin overlay, say of 19-lb. double crown. Some parts require more than one overlay; on this account, and to ensure the overlays being exactly where needed, all the overlaying is not done on this tympan sheet, but a clean tympan sheet (pasted at the four corners) is put over the whole. Two impressions follow, one on tissue paper and one on the clean tympan sheet. From the tissue pull all the high parts are cut out, and also a small cut-out slit made close to the border corners so that it can be placed accurately on the tympan sheet; but before fixing the tissue overlay the gauge must be marked. Taking a sheet of its own paper, the edge of the sheet is laid flush to the lower side of the impression on the tympan, and far enough to the left to show the full width of the printing; then the upper edge of the sheet is turned back to the upper side of the border and folded. By lowering the sheet till the fold is in line with the upper side of the border the exact centre is of course obtained. Trimming—a pica at

---

[a] "Presswork," by Wm. J. Kelly.

front and a nonpareil extra at foot—has to be allowed for so that the fold is put beyond the edge of the printing in each case to the extent desired. The quads for the lower gauge will each be about ten ems from the end of the sheet, and the head gauge will be near the centre—a little above rather than below. This is a job in which good register is essential; so having marked the places for the quads, the whole of the packing is cut through and the quads are fastened direct on to the platen with elastic glue. Thus, if it should be necessary at a later stage to alter anything under the tympan, the accuracy of the gauge will not be endangered. For the same reason—the obtaining good register—the gripper fingers (owing to a tendency as they come into contact to slightly move the sheets fed in working) will be fixed so that they fall clear of the sheets, and a piece of thick cardboard fastened inside each to act as a frisket. To ensure sufficient grip to keep the sheets on the tympan as they leave the forme, a piece of cork is stuck on the front of the gripper fingers, an inch or two from the bottom according to the furniture in the forme.

The paper for the job is coated, and on that account a sheet of its own is especially suitable for the top sheet of the make-ready. The two bottom corners are pasted and made fast, and, after the sheet has been drawn tight, the top corners are similarly treated; then an impression is taken on it. Any parts of the rules or border sprays that appear too heavy are effectually treated by scraping away the coating with a knife sufficiently to obtain the desired relief. After regulating the impression, bearing in mind the extra sheet in feeding, a little french chalk is dusted over the tympan to prevent off-set. So that the top sheet does not impede the taking-off, a piece is cut away from the upper side, and then the make-ready is complete.

The next consideration is the colour. As most pressmen know, bronze blue does not take kindly to enamelled and coated papers; therefore a sufficient quantity of colour for the job is put on the mixing slab, and a thin piece of curd soap say, about the size and thickness of a halfpenny for a quarter pound of colour together with a little strong varnish, is thoroughly mixed in. This done, the colour is put in the ductor, discretion being exercised in setting the same to ensure the supply being about right.

Some twenty sheets are now run off on any odd paper large enough and that has two good edges to lay to; these will most probably be wanted in registering the other workings. After running the odd sheets the ductor screws are eased, or tightened, or left alone, according as the colour supply necessitates, and a good impression to submit for approval is taken. The approved example is kept near at hand for occasional comparison—more especially during the first few hundred runs, until the colour supply is perfectly regular. Sheets spoiled in working are not thrown away, but laid on one side in case they may be needed for trying the subsequent workings. As to lay, the sheets are fed to the bottom gauges and gently pushed up to the side gauge.

The second forme is in chocolate. For this colour rollers of a drier nature than those used for bronze blue are best. Green or tacky rollers would not carry the right amount of colour.

This is a lighter forme than the first, so that the third tympan sheet can be dispensed with; but an overlay will be needed for the heavy scroll border. Before cutting the overlay, however, a pull is taken on the tympan sheet, a small triangular piece cut out of each border corner of a good sheet of the blue forme, and the sheet placed over the impression on the tympan: the border corners being cut away discloses when it is in exact register, and the correct lay thus indicated is marked and the quads are fixed accordingly. The registering of the forme follows. How many of the odd sheets will be required for this purpose depends mostly upon the skill of the compositor. When the forme registers, the odd sheets remaining are run off for future use, and an impression is also taken on thin double crown—about 19-lb. for the overlay. From this sheet all the light parts of the scroll border and other parts not required are cut away, leaving only the solid background of the border; this overlay is slightly pasted and fixed in position on the tympan. With these exceptions, the method of operation is fully covered in the foregoing particulars.

The lays for the buff and blue tints are obtained in a similar manner to the chocolate forme. Both the tints are made by mixing with transparent tinting medium: the buff from burnt sienna, the blue from bronze blue. A small quantity of the tinting medium is put on the mixing slab and the colour added by degrees until the desired shade is produced. Tints mixed with white ink give about the same hue on paper as in bulk; but, mixed with tinting medium, to give a tint of the same shade as the buff or blue in question, the bulk would appear about half depth of the full colour.

In the successful working of tints if there is a secret, then it is in having everything scrupulously clean and in using good colours to obtain them. When the make-ready is finished it is a very good plan to clean up a second time before proceeding with the run. A medium quality roller—that is, not too tacky nor too dry—should be used for working tints.

For keeping formes clear in working and for carrying the requisite amount of colour satisfactorily, a combination of two patent rollers to one of ordinary composition is found to be entirely successful.

In a general way, it is very seldom necessary with the better class of work to resort to a softer packing than the one described; but of course according to the quality and condition of the type must the pressman's discretion be exercised. With worn material thinner cardboard and more sheets, and in some cases all sheets, will give better results. For half-tone blocks, however, a still harder packing should be used, say six or eight sheet card with sheets of paper as necessary.

FINE WORK AT CYLINDER MACHINE. As a preliminary to the working of a fine job on this class of machine a few remarks anent the bearings and bearers will not be out of place. First as to the split brass bearings that carry the cylinder. The pressman will do well to examine these occasionally, as it is important they should fit the shaft perfectly; or, in other words, run smoothly without any play. The tendency is, of course, to wear more at the top than at the bottom or sides, and when any unevenness is observable from this cause the bearings should be brought together by carefully filing the shoulders. Then as to the cylinder bearers. Whether of wood or of steel, these must be exactly type high. In the present case they are of wood, and when tested with a four-line metal letter were just a trifle lower than the letter to allow of a piece of type-wrapping or other strong paper being fastened on the face. After a piece of glass paper had been passed two or three times along the face of the bearers, the strips of paper (cut the exact size of face of bearers) were glued and pressed firmly home with a piece of rag. The cylinder was then run over them, the impression of the cylinder closely traced, and any light parts the examination disclosed were made good with the same kind of paper. The object of this paper facing is to obtain a surer adherence of the pieces of brown paper that will later be added, to prevent dipping at the top and bottom of the pages, than could be obtained if these pieces were pasted directly on to the bearers.

Into the question of the unadvisableness of packing the bearers at all it is not intended to enter further than to say that it is altogether inconsistent with the experience of many of the finest American and English pressmen. Whether the bearers are of wood, gun-metal, or steel does not materially affect the point. The fact remains that the cylinder is slightly raised during impression and that there is a consequent drop when released from impression, and unless this is met by packing the bearers either the type or the quality of the work suffers.

The following is the dictum of one whose superb workmanship alone sufficiently demonstrates its value:

> The noise or "bump" between margins may be easily obviated by unscrewing the metal bearers and packing them with paper at the spots between the margins, so that the cylinder will have a uniform strain all along the impression. This will keep the cylinder lifted in action until the impression is completed.*

The forme for working is eight pages of the literary portion of this book, and, the machine having been properly cleaned, the dressing of the cylinder will claim first consideration. On different machines the number of sheets would be regulated to suit the height of the beard of the cylinder; the correct packing is easily ascertained by putting a straight-edge from the beard of the cylinder on to the sheets. The packing will, in this case, consist entirely of sheets of paper, and being a quad crown machine, the first sheet will be one of 72-lb. quad demy.† After turning down about an inch and a quarter the sheet is dampened‡ (not soaked) with a sponge, the turndown is pasted, and the sheet put on the cylinder, damp side outward, in this manner: The cylinder having been turned three-quarters round (so that the grippers are open), the pasted turndown of the sheet is inserted between the grippers and the front of the cylinder; when quite even, two or three inches of the centre of the pasted turndown are made fast, and then, the right hand resting firmly on the centre, with the left hand the sheet is drawn tightly along to the end and the first half of the turndown secured. The other half is similarly treated. The cylinder is then run nearly home (so that the grippers are closed), the end of the sheet turned up and about an inch width pasted all along; but before sticking the sheet down it is gradually drawn round

---

* P. S. M. Munro, *American Pressman*, No. 3; Vol. IV.

† The object in having the first sheet as large, or nearly as large, as the cylinder will take is that it prevents unnecessary cleaning off. In the event of more formes of the work following, or even other work of a similar class, a new sheet would not be required.

‡ Care is taken to avoid dampening the turndown, lest it should not withstand the strain of drawing the sheet tight.

to fit the cylinder without wrinkle. This is effectually done by pressing the sheet to the cylinder with the palm of the hand, beginning at the gripper edge centre and working by degrees from the middle of the sheet to the outer edges right round to the pasted leaving end of the sheet.

A few minutes is sufficient time for the first sheet to dry, and then six sheets of 30-lb. double crown are taken, half an inch of the front edges turned down, and the turndown of each slightly pasted. These having been put in place securely and free from crease, a sheet of double royal of about the same thickness is dampened, pasted, and applied in precisely the same manner as the first sheet.

As is well known, with dampened sheets there is liability to shrinkage from the sides, oftentimes to the detriment of the make-ready. To obviate this it is a very good plan to put on either side of the tympan sheet a strip of paper about three inches in width and long enough to reach from the gripper edge to the end of the tympan sheet. The strips should be dampened one side and pasted the other, and affixed partly on the tympan sheet and partly on the cylinder. They are best put on by gentle outward pressure, using a piece of rag to prevent them from bursting. The ends of the cylinder should also first be cleaned with emery cloth to ensure the adherence of the strips.

The dressing of the cylinder is now finished. While the drying of the top sheet is in progress the forme is put up and—there being no present necessity of testing the foundations of the pressroom—gently lowered on to the bed of the machine with signature to the ink slab. Of course a gauge is kept of the pitch, so that with a sheet of its own paper folded and laid in position on the forme, and allowing a great primer for take-up, the requisite furniture is put in, the lock-up bar and quoins are placed (the quoins being sufficiently tightened with the fingers to keep the forme from shifting), and then the forme is planed down.

As there is nothing in this forme that calls for great rolling power, four inkers and two riders will be ample in this connection. To adjust

St. Bride Foundation Institute, Bride Lane, Fleet Street, E.C.

THE GOVERNORS of the **ST. BRIDE FOUNDATION** beg to announce that they have made arrangements for **COURSES OF INSTRUCTION** in

Letterpress Printing  DURING THE WINTER SEASON.

Commencing for COMPOSITORS IN OCTOBER, AND FOR MACHINE MANAGERS & PRESSMEN IN NOVEMBER.

Printing Schools Committee:

Mr. C. J. DRUMMOND, *Chairman.*
REV. E. C. HAWKINS, M.A., *Ex-Officio.*
Mr. JOHN T. BEDFORD, *Deputy.*
Mr. EDMUND W. EVANS.
Mr. C. AUSTEN LEIGH.
Mr. ROBERT T. PRATT.
Mr. T. C. ST. ANDREW ST. JOHN.
Mr. J. FARLOW WILSON.

VALUABLE PRIZES Are offered by the City and Guilds of London Institute to Students attending Technical Classes.

these, the ink slab is run far enough in to take the rollers on and the side nuts of the roller bearings are loosened. With the rollers thus resting on the slab, the riders are screwed down and the inkers pressed up closely, but not tightly, to them. After adjusting, the riders and inkers are lifted (the latter with the foot lift), and a small quantity of ink is put on the wavers and run up. Two inkers will suffice during make-ready; therefore the other two are taken off, their position being duly noted so that they shall be replaced in the same brackets.

By this time the top sheet on the cylinder is thoroughly dry, and an impression is taken on a sheet of its own paper to see that the pages are in the centre. The correct position obtained, a sheet is properly backed, and the compositor makes any alterations required in the make-up to ensure register. Another sheet of its own paper with two sheets of 30-lb. double crown (the three sheets run through together) gives an impression full enough to indicate the parts that would be best brought up by underlaying. Parenthetically, the exact position of the forme is noted before raising for the purpose of underlaying, and after the underlaying is accomplished the forme is securely fastened on the machine from the sides with two pieces of double broad, placed parallel and quoined up, as well as by locking up at the bar.

Now to pack the bearers. This requires six pieces of rather stout brown paper, cut to the exact width of the bearers: the four for the take-up and leaving ends are about two inches long, and the pieces for the space in the head about a pica longer than that space. After being pasted, these are accurately placed by putting the straight-edge in line with the pages. The centre packing extends about a nonpareil each way over the actual margin, and the end packing is allowed to encroach about a similar amount at the bottom of the pages.

Two impressions follow, one on the tympan sheet and another on thin double crown with two sheets of 30-lb. at the back. From the thin sheet all the pages are cut out, close to the edge and minus the

P

head-line and rule and the bottom line. These "cut-outs" are thinly and evenly pasted all over, and each is duly fixed on the corresponding page on the tympan. Some pressmen recommend pasting only the front edge of this kind of overlay. Both methods have been tried. When the edge only is pasted, during running these overlays are liable to be forced back out of place, in addition to which there is tendency to crease at the leaving end. Carefully pasted all over, they adhere firmly to the tympan.

The next pull is on a sheet of its own with one sheet at the back. Any parts defective are touched up with tissue paper, and then comes the final sheet of the make-ready. Mention was made in the Platen work section of the utility of a top sheet of coated paper, and for the same reason a sheet of its own will now be used. Half-an-inch is turned down and pasted, and the sheet is put on; then three strips of strong paper, about three inches wide and nine inches long, dampened one side and half-an-inch pasted at the end of the other side, are attached (one in the centre and one near each side) to the leaving end of the sheet. The centre strip is put on first: keeping the pasted end firmly on the sheet with one hand, the other hand is passed along the strip to within about an inch of the end, and that portion is turned up, pasted, and made fast to the tympan sheet. The other strips are similarly applied, and as they dry the top sheet is drawn perfectly taut. When the strips are dry, two impressions are taken, one on the coated tympan sheet and one on a sheet of its own paper. What final touches are necessary can be readily discerned from this sheet—the parts too strong are relieved by scraping the coating, while the weak parts are touched up with water colour.[*] A few waste sheets are then run through and the make-ready is finished.

Before starting, however, there is another rather important operation to perform, and that is the cutting of the vibrator, which transfers the

---

[*] See page 99 for mode of preparing the colour.

ink from the reciprocating distributing cylinder to the slab, to ensure the supply being just where it is needed. With work of an ordinary description of course it would not be necessary to cut a vibrator; but for high-class work of long numbers or with several formes of pages of uniform size it is advisable. The wavers are therefore lifted and the slab is run under the ink ductor. A waste sheet of paper is put on the slab and the vibrator placed on the sheet in direct line with the vibrator brackets. Then it is rolled along the slab on to the forme, the pages of which leave their mark on its face, thus giving a correct indication of the parts to be cut away. The purpose of the sheet of paper on the slab is now evident. The cutting away is done in a slanting direction and extends about a nonpareil beyond the page limits, the parts between the pages being taken out so that the space somewhat resembles a V; but in no part does the cut reach to the stock, for the very good reason that a roller does not always adhere in every part to the stock.

When the ductor vibrator has been put in, the wavers and inkers replaced, the ductor supplied with ink and set, and a few waste sheets run through, the printing of the bulk is proceeded with.

MAKING READY HALF-TONE ENGRAVINGS.—To what a remarkable extent the printing of process blocks has entered the "daily round" of the pressman, a great—possibly the greater—portion of modern typographical production testifies. Like his American *confrère*, the British "printer-man" has not been without the advice of those who advocate that "the least done to the photo-engraver's work the better," and, moreover, that overlaying "is often, if not generally, a mistake," not giving results equal to the first press proof. Unfortunately for the recommendation, the work produced under its influence is not such as to gain a craftsman's respect. Mr. W. J. Kelly has made us familiar with the proof-puller's method; but the engraver's proof-puller with his hand-press and "dwell" impression to give effect to underlays immediately beneath the plate and backed up by an iron bed, and the pressman with the plate fastened on a wooden mount (oftentimes uneven and out of square) on a cylinder or platen machine, are working under conditions so totally different as not to admit of comparison. Yet, given suitable rollers, ink, and paper, the skilful pressman's work is very seldom inferior to the proof-puller's. To show the absurdity of the comparison it is only necessary to point out that while the pressman's method must be that which is most suitable for the production of thousands of copies, the proof-puller's only concern is to get some half-dozen good examples. And it is pretty certain that if the pressman's rate of production had only been equal to the proof-puller's, photo-engraving would hardly have become, "with the single exception of portraiture, the most important application of photography." Until the pressman is provided with mounts of a harder substance than the wood at present in use, together with an easy mode of unmounting and mounting, to obtain satisfactory results he must perforce exercise his ingenuity *over* as well as *under* the block. But even with an improved method of mounting it does not follow that all process blocks could be successfully printed without overlays; for neither of the two following reasons why half-tones require overlays would be affected by the substance of the mount. They are both taken from the *American Pressman,* and will thoroughly accord with the experience of most, if not all, pressmen who are intimately acquainted with first-class process work.

> One of the secrets which so many writers who presume to instruct the craft have failed to discover is, that without an overlay the mesh of a half-tone plate pulls away the coating of the fine-surfaced papers on which half-tones are printed—a small quantity from each sheet, so infinitesimal in some papers as to be beyond detection until a number have been printed. In time, however, this accumulation betrays itself, and the half-tone then behaves in a way puzzling to the one who does not know. It is here that the overlay gets in its fine, enduring work. It applies just enough pressure to drive the ink on to and slightly into the paper, preventing accumulation of flock, and securing sharpness and permanence of impression.
>
> The blending effect produced by the introduction of this screen or film unfortunately interferes with the sudden or contrasting effects which the

artist sometimes intends, and makes them appear much flatter in the reproduction than in the original. This is where the skill of the pressman comes into play. It is his duty to restore to the cut, by proper treatment with an overlay, the contrasts and tonings which the drawing has lost during its reproduction, and which are essential to the harmony of the whole.

A suitable dressing of the cylinder for a forme containing half-tone blocks would be precisely similar to that given in detail in the "Fine Work at Cylinder Machine" section.

Assuming that the pressman has to deal with a forme, say, of sixteen pages, containing both blocks and type, to be printed on coated paper, the first matter of importance is the *Underlaying of the Blocks*, and in this connection a hint is necessary as to the material used in levelling up. The millboard,* card, or paper used for this purpose should be hard and even in substance. As all blocks with wood mounts yield slightly to hard packing according to the surface presented for impression, the blocks should be underlaid until they stand a trifle higher than the type, say to the extent of a sheet of 21-lb. wove. All the underlays should be nearly flush with the edges of the mount. Usually the first pull of a process block shows a rather heavier impression at the edges than in the central part; but as underlays smaller than the mount are likely to cause a rocking motion of the block, it is better to supply the pressure from the top. If, however, the central hollowness is more than slight, the plate should be taken off and the deficiency made good by underlaying the plate; also if there is enough unevenness of mount to cause rocking, it is best treated by taking off the plate and rubbing down the uneven part with sand-paper. To repeat Kelly's words: "Skilful underlaying is the key to good presswork," and that is pre-eminently true in respect of process blocks. After the underlaying has been done,

---

* The fact that pressmen are oftentimes compelled to use millboard—frequently two thicknesses—in order to bring blocks up to type level, ought to suggest to photo-engravers generally that the height of their mounting material is not all that could be desired. Every pressman would rather have a block a little too low than too high; but the sixtieth part of an inch below type height would be more preferable than a sixteenth, to put it moderately.

its effect is tested by taking an impression for examination in the usual way, and the finishing touches are added as required.

The *Adjustment of the Rollers* for process blocks should be very carefully attended to. Selecting rollers of a firm but live (that is, slightly tacky) nature and of as true surface as possible, they should be adjusted to ensure fair rolling without dipping into the face of the forme. Too heavy rolling and dipping of rollers involve loss of time by causing frequent stoppages for washing up.

Having taken an impression on the tympan sheet, it is now in order to ascertain what *Overlaying* is needed in the central parts of the blocks to make up the slight deficiencies of pressure. This is done by taking a pull on a sheet of its own paper with two sheets about equal to 30-lb. double crown at the back and overlaying the low parts with two or three thicknesses of tissue paper, varying the size according to the requirements. As these overlays have a spreading effect, they should of course be smaller than the part it is desired to bring up.

When even impression has been obtained, two pulls are taken on paper of smooth quality, equal to 19-lb. and 23-lb. double crown respectively, for the *Overlays*. The pressman would probably find that amongst the sixteen blocks there would be three degrees of tones: some would be almost entirely light, others with medium and light tones, and others, again, with light, medium, and dark tones. In this event, the overlays would be of three kinds. For the light blocks, take the impression on the 23-lb. paper, and, holding the knife slanting inwards (so that the overlay has a slight bevel), cut just inside the edges of the picture. For the blocks with medium tones, also take the impression on the 23-lb. paper and cut out all the high lights (that is, the extremely light parts) of the picture. Proceed in precisely the same manner with the third kind of block up to and including the cutting out of the high lights, then take the impression on the 19-lb. paper, cut out the dark parts, paste slightly, and affix them in place on the 23-lb. overlay. When the overlays are ready, paste them slightly all over and put them accurately in place on the tympan. The reiteration of the injunction to "paste slightly" will be noted; it is important, so let that fact excuse its repetition.

Another sheet of thin but good quality "printing" should now be put on the cylinder. This sheet should correspond in size to the top sheet of the cylinder dressing, and be dampened and affixed in the usual way. Two more strips, about an inch and a half in width, to prevent side shrinkage of this sheet, should also be applied in the manner already described.

When this sheet is dry, take two more impressions: one on a sheet of its own paper (with one sheet of ordinary printing quality at the back) and one on the new tympan sheet. The impression on the coated paper would disclose what parts are too harsh—most probably the edges of the pictures—and the necessary relief could be given, according to the degree of harshness indicated, either by cutting out, paring with a sharp knife, or rubbing down with an ink eraser. The inequalities of the surrounding type would also be made good by patching up on this sheet. Take another impression to test the effect of the treatment, and make good any defective parts.

The final sheet for the cylinder follows next: a sheet of its own coated paper. Fasten the leaving edge of this sheet with three strips (similar to those mentioned in the previous example) to draw the sheet taut, taking care to paste the ends before dampening the strips and to affix them as far on the coated sheet as the margin will allow. When the strips are dry, take an impression on this final sheet. The operations of taking from or adding to the tones of the blocks require delicate manipulation. The merest scrape of the coating is sufficient to give relief; and a slight covering of water colour, put on with a camel hair brush, is enough to intensify the dark tones.

As to the water colour. A perfectly smooth and suitable preparation can be made by soaking for ten or twelve hours, in just sufficient water to cover, say a dozen ordinary moist colours. Pour off the water not absorbed, add about a teaspoonful of fish glue, and thoroughly mix. If bottled it will keep for a considerable length of time, and also be convenient to take the quantity needed for the particular work in hand.

For working half-tones the ink cannot be too good, but it can be too stiff. An ink of medium consistency will be found most satisfactory in running. In the case of coated stock, stiff ink causes trouble by pulling off the face of the paper and a consequent filling up of the mesh of the blocks. At the present time there are several very good reducing agents in the market, and by using ink of extra good quality reduced to a free working consistency by one of these media the results will be generally successful.

MAKING READY WOOD ENGRAVINGS.—For a forme containing electros from wood engravings, the packing would not be so hard as that used for half-tone blocks. The usual linen would form the foundation of the dressing, followed by some half-dozen sheets of good paper —say equal to 30-lb. double crown—according to the beard of the cylinder. The turndown (about a quarter of an inch) of these sheets should be pasted in places sufficiently to prevent them slipping back. Over these put the large tympan sheet, dampened and applied in the manner already set forth, also adding the strips to save side shrinkage.

Here, again, careful *Underlaying* is essential. Get the blocks as nearly perfectly level as possible, and underlay them until they stand a very little above the height of the type. Treat cases of distinct irregularity of surface by unmounting and underlaying the plate; on this account it will be an advantage if the electros are screwed on.

The engravings should be quite clean, and where turps does not effect the desired cleanliness a little creosote can be applied. Allow the antiseptic a few minutes to do its work, then brush the face of the cut and wipe dry with a piece of rag.

Address:
58, FARRINGDON STREET, LONDON.

Reproduced from a Water-colour Drawing by
JOHN MEAD & SONS **Photo-chromotype Process**
in Five Printings.

Assuming the work in hand to be of a first-class character and requiring *Three-Sheet Overlays* for the blocks, three impressions would be taken on good quality (that is, smooth) printing paper about equal to 30-lb., 23-lb., and 19-lb. double crown respectively, with as little ink as will show clearly all the details of the engraving. Take first the impression on the 30-lb. paper, and after clipping out the illustration proceed to cut out the high lights (in other words, the white and extremely light parts) of the engraving as indicated in example No. 1 (which is a reproduction of an actual foundation overlay), together with any fading edges the illustration may contain.

No. 1. THE FOUNDATION OF THE OVERLAY WITH HIGH LIGHTS CUT OUT.

It may be well to mention that in cutting overlays the knife should be held aslant. In all cases of gradation of perspective — that is, solid shading off to heavy lines and heavy lines to fine lines; the base of the sechommeter here shown furnishes an example of both the cutting should be done so as to give the overlay a slight bevel, which will preserve the continuity of tone.

The next proceeding is to cut out the solids and affix them to the foundation sheet. It is not an uncommon mode to leave the solids till last; but there are two very good reasons for putting them next to the foundation sheet: (1) the small pieces are kept more securely in place;

(2) the harmonious relation of light and shade is not liable to suffer from abruptness. For the solids the impression on the 19-lb. paper is used.

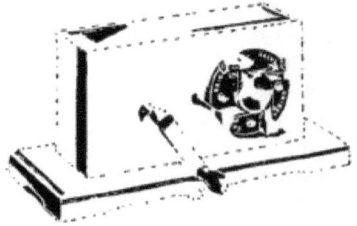

No. 2. THE SOLIDS.

In order to obtain the gradations essential to perspective, the wood engraver employs, in addition to high lights and solids, degrees of lines which can generally be divided into two classes: fine or light lines and heavy or dark lines. To enhance the perspective of these lines is the

No. 3. FINAL SHEET, WITH FINE LINES OR SECONDS CUT OUT.

office of the third sheet of the overlay. Take the pull on the 23-lb. paper, cut out the high lights and fine lines, leaving the solids and heavy lines to form the final sheet of the overlay; after slightly pasting, put it — or the various parts, as the case may be — in place on the foundation sheet.

Accuracy in putting the different parts of the solids and seconds on the foundation sheet, as well as in putting the completed overlay on the tympan, is important in the highest degree.

After fixing the overlays, put on a clean, dampened tympan sheet. When the new tympan sheet is dry, it is in order to attend to the type portion of the forme. An impression on the tympan sheet will show that the overlays have to some extent taken the pressure off the type, and this should be made good by overlaying with a rather thin printing paper of good quality, finally touching up any weak parts with tissue paper.

No. 4.   WITH THREE-SHEET OVERLAY.

If the various operations have been skilfully executed the job should now present a finished appearance, and only require the final sheet to protect the make-ready. This sheet is dampened and applied in the usual way, and while it is drying such matters as cleaning up, if the sheet is to be worked in colour, and putting the ink in the ductor should be attended to, taking care not to run a single sheet until the make-ready is perfectly dry.

In a general way, it would not be necessary to cut a three-sheet overlay for engravings as small as the one here given in illustration of the principle of cutting the various parts to suit the degrees of light and shade in engravings. Four and five sheet overlays are sometimes used with excellent effect in special work. But in cutting all overlays the pressman will obtain the most satisfactory results by first considering the character of the engraving and then endeavouring to carry out the idea of the artist.

For medium quality work, a *Two-Sheet Overlay* will suffice. In this class of overlay the special sheet for the solids is omitted; but the gradations of tone are fairly successfully preserved by cutting out both the high lights and the seconds on a rather larger scale than that adopted in the case of a three-sheet overlay.

To cut a *One-Sheet Overlay* entails but a small expenditure of time. The improved appearance, however, of printed work with only a one-sheet overlay, in which the high lights and fading edges have been cut away on the larger scale, over that of work done without an overlay well repays for the time spent in cutting. For a one-sheet overlay the heaviest paper — the 30-lb. — would be used.

Although the foregoing methods of making ready half-tones and woodcuts have been taken in their cylinder machine aspects, the principles of underlaying and overlaying, together with the remarks on the ink and the application of the water-colour preparation, hold equally good, as the pressman will readily perceive, in the case of platen machine work.

EMBOSSING. In the enhancement of certain classes of fine job work the embossing of suitable border bands, sprays, and ornaments, or head and tail pieces, is a very useful auxiliary. Various methods are now in vogue for accomplishing embossed effects, and the pressman will do well to make himself acquainted, if not practically then theoretically, with at least one of these methods.

For rapidity of preparation, sheet gutta percha, heated and placed on the platen and then firmly impressed with the embossing forme, can be recommended. The matrix thus produced will be ready for working on within five minutes of fixing; the embossment, too, is very well defined, and after a run of three thousand no difference has been perceptible either in height or sharpness.

The following method was adopted in the production of the example in this work, except that plaster of paris was used in place of barytes powder. Plaster of paris mixed with flour paste makes a very satisfactory preparation for the matrix. One precaution is necessary, however, if plaster of paris is used—it should be of fine and smooth quality.

> In the first place, the embossing plate or border was locked in a chase ready for the press. Then the forme was "made ready" so that the impression showed firmly and evenly on the tympan, without the use of ink. Then a paste was made of barytes powder and a good flour paste thoroughly mixed in equal proportions, the flour paste being free from lumps. Then the face of the forme was well oiled, so that when the impression was taken the pasted sheet would not stick to it. Then the paste was spread evenly and thinly over the impression on the tympan with a stiff brush, and a sheet of manilla tissue was laid over this, and an impression taken upon it. Then this impression was again coated thinly with the paste, care being taken to put the paste where it was most needed, and another sheet of the tissue was added. This operation was repeated until every part of the work was embossed as evenly as the plate or border would allow. Then the matrix so made was dried with a hot iron or a piece of burning paper; in the meantime, at intervals of a minute or two, a half-dozen impressions were taken on the tympan so that the matrix would not warp or shrink out of position while being dried. After the matrix was thoroughly hard and dry, the guides were set and the sheets run through.*

This method also has simplicity as well as effectualness to its recommendation:

> There is no limit to form; a plain rule can be made to emboss as well as a border, either in straight bands, or in curves or squares, diamonds or oblongs. We have framed in our strips or bands with a border of sand-paper pasted on a piece of electro blocking, and printed dry.
>
> In working, the embossing bands can be of type metal or rule, or an electrotype can be made, depending upon the number to be printed and

---

* The "Colour Printer," by J. F. Earhart.

the hardness and thickness of the stock to be embossed. If a very deep impression is required, it is best to have a female cast made of papier maché, well beaten in. For light embossing, however, a thick piece of blotting paper fastened down on the tympan sheet will answer all purposes. This should be well dampened, then a heavy well-packed impression taken, and left on the impression for awhile until it sets. A little oil on the face of the forme will prevent any sticking of the blotter or papier maché. When the blotter is fairly dry, the pins can be set and the sheet adjusted to its place, and fed dry without rollers in the press.[*]

The most successful examples of embossed work can be obtained on stout paper of the cartridge class with intaglio ornaments and borders—in other words, where the design is surrounded by a solid ground.

TREATMENT OF ROLLERS.—It is becoming somewhat hackneyed to say that the condition of his rollers is an all-important matter to the pressman. But would remarks on the treatment of rollers be complete without it? "Good rollers will do good work in the hands of an ordinary man; but a skilful pressman cannot do good work with inferior rollers," says Kelly. "You can have the best presses, new type, and a skilful pressman, yet with inferior rollers you cannot produce the best work," avers Morgan; and possibly every pressman of observation, even if he has not given expression to corresponding dicta, is fully convinced of their truth from his own experience.

Climate, with its variations of heat and cold, moisture and dryness, is admittedly the cause of most of the pressman's trouble from his rollers. A roller may work excellently one day, and yet the next day the pressman's ingenuity may be taxed to the utmost in getting that same roller to work satisfactorily. And as the pressman fortunately cannot control the climate, and as there is not a roller yet made that will withstand for any lengthened period all weathers and still keep its working qualities, it is well that he should turn his attention to the best means of treatment when atmospheric changes have impaired those

---

[*] *American Art Printer*, No. 5; Vol. II., 1888.

working qualities. It is not suggested that the recommendations here set forth are the best possible; but they are offered as having been applied with some degree of success.

Take the case of *Hard Rollers* first. Rollers as often become hard from improper washing as from dry or frosty weather. They may have been washed off with benzine "not wisely, but too well," and too often, and thus the suction has been destroyed, and the face has become dry and cracked. On this account benzine is not a good thing for cleaning rollers; and the pressman, knowing how much the excellence of his work depends on the suitable elasticity of his rollers, will do well to see that it is seldom if ever used for that purpose. Paraffin, turps, and, in some cases, weak lye are all preferable to benzine for washing rollers. To restore temporary suction to a hard roller, however—that is the point. Take a small quantity of glycerine and rub it well into the face; when dry, a second dose should be administered. Before putting it on the machine, a coating of compound made by pouring a pint of boiling water on a quarter-pound of powdered alum and two ounces of brown sugar, and stirring till dissolved, will enhance the treatment. The compound should of course be cold when applied, and as it is useful for rollers in another state (shortly to be mentioned), it is handy if kept in a bottle.

Then there are *Green Rollers,* in other words, rollers that have absorbed too much moisture, and consequently will not take ink. This applies chiefly to patent rollers, in the manufacture of which glycerine has an important place. In an excellent article on "Roller Composition" that appeared in the *American Bookmaker* a few years ago, Mr. R. J. Morgan says:

> The peculiar properties of glycerine are: that it never freezes at any temperature, and, consequently, heat or cold has little effect upon its consistency; that—a very important property—it never evaporates; and, that it has a very powerful attraction for moisture, and will gain notably in weight if exposed to the air. This last property is rather a disadvantage,

and is the cause of all the trouble attendant upon the use of glycerine in rollers. It is this property which makes rollers to some extent dependent in quality upon the variations of the weather. Roller makers say: "Give us a substance having all the qualities of glycerine, except its attraction for moisture, and we will give you an almost perfect roller."

When a roller is green and wanted for immediate use, it can be much improved by first washing in turps and then rubbing a little powdered alum into the face, afterwards wiping off clean. If the roller supply is good, the pressman may be able to put on one side for a day or two a roller that is found to be green; if before putting in the roller cupboard it is first cleaned in turps and rubbed down a few times—say at intervals of about two hours—with the compound (which is alike good for either patent or glue and molasses rollers), its condition will be found greatly improved.

As to the *Seasoning of Rollers*. New rollers should have time to become fairly set before being put on the machine, otherwise their life will in all probability be a short one. It is not always possible, however, to give rollers seasoning time, and, when this is the case, it is a very good plan to clean off the oil, rub them well with turps, and give them at least an hour's grace. Seasoning cannot be restricted to a stated period—it is entirely a matter of damp or dry weather—and a practised touch is required to decide when a roller has attained that degree of combined toughness and elasticity best suited to a lengthened service.

The foregoing constitute the leading features of fine presswork. It is evident that the would-be successful artist pressman must be a "man of parts." To use the gist of a well-known aphorism, it is expedient that he should know *something* about many things and *much* about some things; but indispensable that he should know *all* that is worth knowing about one thing, and that is the machine entrusted to his care. Perhaps nothing is more essential in forming the basis of his technical knowledge than a thorough understanding of its construction and principles. It will be the right groundwork for the reception of the other craftsmanlike accomplishments, the possession and proper application of which alone are calculated to realise that "consciousness of a power and mastery" consequent on the knowing how to do things in exactly the right way.

The French have a proverb which in effect says that no man is indispensable. In its ultimity the proverb is of course incontrovertible. But as far as Fine Printing is concerned, the competent artist pressman of to-day can lay a very near claim to that quality.

APPENDIX.

In the hope of making this work interesting to the craftsman, and as valuable an object lesson as possible to the typographical student, it has been deemed expedient to append a list of the various colours and tints used in the production of the supplements, sub-titles, and headpieces. In cases of more than one working, the colours are enumerated in the order in which they were printed.

It may also be mentioned that not any part of the work has either been pressed or rolled, every example and sheet, without exception, being as it came from the pressman.

Sub-Titles. Art brown No. 2.

Headpieces and Initials.—Steel blue, reduced with transparent tinting medium.

Frontispiece. Green black, small quantity of strong varnish mixed in.

Circular of 1877. Carmine; black.

Specimen of Wood Engraving.—Black, with a little bronze blue.

Ornamental Panel Style.—Art brown No. 3; tint from burnt sienna with tinting medium.

Typical German Style.—Bronze blue, with addition of a little curd soap and strong varnish to suit the coated paper; chocolate; buff tint from burnt sienna; blue tint from bronze blue—both with tinting medium.

Typical American Style.—After some twenty copies of the key forme had been pulled for registering: pale salmon tint, equal parts of bismarck brown and burnt sienna; lemon tint from yellow chrome; blue tint from bronze blue; grey tint, equal parts of black and bronze blue—all with tinting medium; carnation red; black. The well-defined buff tint in the circle is produced by overlapping the salmon tint with the lemon tint.

British New Style, 1888.—Grey, one-third green black and two-thirds white; light brown, equal parts umber and orange; crimson lake.

Two Half-tone Engravings.—Black, with a little bronze blue.

"Azaleas": Chromo-Typography. Buff ground tint, from chocolate and cobalt blue with tinting medium; yellow; burnt umber; light grey, from white, cobalt blue, madder, and burnt umber; pink, from madder lake with tinting medium; medium green; crimson madder; dark grey, from cobalt blue and scarlet madder with tinting medium.

Geometrical Arrangement of Rule and Border.—Photo brown; rose red; moss green; tint from burnt sienna with tinting medium.

Grouping Display.—Agate; grey, one-third green black and two-thirds white.

Specimen of Embossing.—Navy blue, reduced with tinting medium; buff tint from burnt sienna. The centre spray of the embossing is from an ordinary poster embellishment. The paper is not quite suitable for embossing purposes, owing to its softness; and in addition to this, the embossment has been somewhat flattened in the binding of the work.

Specimen of Swain's Photo-Chromotype.—Lemon chrome, with a little yellow chrome; flesh tint, equal parts carmine and yellow, reduced with tinting medium; antwerp blue, reduced with tinting medium; red, equal parts geranium, deep geranium, and yellow; black.

By permission of LAFAYETTE. Reproduced from a Photograph.

www.ingramcontent.com/pod-product-compliance
Lightning Source LLC
Chambersburg PA
CBHW030344170426
43202CB00010B/1234